STAND UP

Making Peer Pressure Work for You

BILL SANDERS

Fleming H. Revell
A Division of Baker Book House
Grand Rapids, Michigan 49506

Published by Fleming H. Revell
a division of Baker Book House Company
P.O. Box 6287, Grand Rapids, MI 49516-6287

Printed in the United States of America

Library of Congress Cataloging-in-Publication Data

Sanders, Bill, 1951–
    Stand up : making peer pressure work for you / Bill Sanders.
        p.   cm.
    Summary: Gives advice to teenagers on using Christian principles to help them take a stand against harmful peer pressure.
    ISBN 0-8007-5458-1
    1. Peer pressure in adolescence—Juvenile literature. 2. Teenagers—Religious life—Juvenile literature. 3. Sexual ethics—Juvenile literature. [1. Peer pressure. 2. Conduct of life. 3. Christian life.] I. Title.
HQ799.2.P44S26   1993
303.3'27--dc20   93-18504

STAND UP

Other Books for Teens by Bill Sanders

Life, Sex, and Everything in Between
Outtakes: Devotions for Girls
Outtakes: Devotions for Guys
Goalposts: Devotions for Girls
Goalposts: Devotions for Guys
Tough Turf: A Teen Survival Manual
Stand Tall: Learning How to Really Love Yourself

Throughout my life the Lord has strategically placed special encouragers in my path to help me STAND UP to negative peer pressure and be all I can be.

During my high school years, one extraordinary friend was my greatest guide. Steve McKinley taught me to STAND TALL, STAND UP, and STAND OUT. When I goofed up, he quickly forgot it and encouraged me to reach out for more of life.

At the beginning of my career, Bill Uffelman was at the helm of pushing me further and further to believe that I could be a difference-maker through the spoken word. He taught me to STAND UP and try something different when the critics said it couldn't be done.

Now that I am a maturing Christian husband and father, another dear friend has taught me to be "pure for sure" and not to entertain sin, even for a moment. Jacob Aranza has touched countless lives, including mine. He continually teaches me to "Flee, Brother, Flee" when sin is near.

Without such committed friends, I would never have believed I had an exciting and fulfilling future ahead of me. I certainly wouldn't have stood up for myself.

Contents

Acknowledgments

S pecial thanks to Kim Rowan for reading and making so many good suggestions on what I thought was the finished manuscript. Her keen insight has made this a better book.

As always, I thank Kathy Reisner, my sister-like friend who has been typing my books and working side by side with me for many years.

Enjoying the Price

Y ou've got a great future ahead of you, so STAND UP for yourself!

You're going to see those words over and over again in this book because I want you to think about them, feel them, and believe them. Here it goes again . . . Your future can be bright if you'll try with all your might to STAND UP for yourself.

Did you catch the rhyme, the second time? As you read chapter after chapter and listen to story after story, remember that this book is for and about you! You are the only you that can do what God placed you here to do. That's worth repeating as well. You are the only you that can do what God placed you here to do! But you won't do it unless you learn to make peer pressure work for you, not against you, and STAND UP for yourself.

STAND UP for goodness. STAND UP for right. If a cause is just or noble or honest, you could be the one to endorse it, to fight for it, and to make it happen. STAND UP for you! If a party is wrong, if what your friends are doing is unethical, if drugs are presented to you, or if you have the chance to catch a sexually transmitted disease in one easy half-hour of pleasure, I want you to STAND UP for yourself and get out of there!

Remember this little ditty, "If there's trouble near, I'm outta here."

Jacob Aranza teaches me to STAND UP for my Lord, for myself, and for what's right. We were both in a hottub after four days of doing assemblies and evening rallies and we were dead tired. There we were, both happily married, in this hottub at our hotel when two beautiful babes walked in toward us. He grabbed my hand, made me stand up, and as he dragged me out of the hottub, right past those women, he yelled out, "Flee, brother, flee!" Then he said, "We can't be looking at hamburg on the road while there's prime rib waiting at home!"

Now a look at reality. Some people say my "flee" story means living like a nun in a convent. They say "You mean you can't even be in a hottub with another woman?" I say it's not a hard and fast rule, but here is a truth for me that's hard and fast: If I don't entertain even the thought of another woman, my marriage will last much longer than if I look for hottubs full of beautiful ladies and jump in. It's the same with you. You must beware of danger zones or possible trouble spots and stand up and leave. On the other hand, at times we must stay and stand up for the truth. We'll know deep in our hearts that we made a difference in this world, even if we can't see the difference at the time. For example, there was the time I made my first national appearance on NBC.

Barely a week before the taping, the producer for "A Closer Look with Faith Daniels" had called me and asked what I would say to parents who let their teens have sex in their homes. As someone who speaks to teens across the country and hears from them when they hurt, I gave it to her straight. I pointed out the mistakes parents made when they gave in. Then I described the three thousand letters I'd received in the past year from teens who told of the pain and heartache they felt from having sex with partners who were here today and gone tomorrow. I told of the many letters I get concerning post-abortion trauma and of the agony of having to tell a spouse on the honeymoon that they've already had other sex partners, that they didn't save themselves for marriage.

She told me I'd be perfect for the show and that she would send me the plane tickets.

Excited as I was, I knew enough to spend the next four days preparing. I wanted to have the knowledge that would help people understand the importance of making the right decision. Many parents and teens would watch the show, and my words might carry a lot of weight. I had to stand up for what I believe and trust that even one life might be touched.

A few days later, I got to New York. A limo picked me up at the airport. On the way to the studio, I told the driver about the show and about my stand against letting teens do whatever they want, wherever they want to.

"What would you do if your daughter told you she was going to have sex anyway? Would you kick her out of the house?" he asked.

"What would you do if your daughter was into drugs, using crack cocaine?" I countered. "Would you get her more drugs—or would you get her help?"

As he let me out at Rockefeller Center, he told me I was taking a tough stand.

Did I realize how tough it was going to be?

Inside the studio, I met some other people who would be on the show, but none of us were introduced to those who supported teens having sex in the home.

They didn't want us to get into a heated discussion before the show began.

For the first half of the show, guests talked about how much better it was for a child to have sex inside the home than out of it. The audience applauded a father who took this stand. He and his daughter had an agreement. She could bring her boyfriends home for sex if he could bring his girlfriends home for sex. His daughter praised him, saying that she could communicate with her dad, while other sexually active teens could not.

When my turn to speak came, only two short segments were left. I only had a few minutes and wanted to make them count. From their reactions to the earlier part of the show, I knew that at least three-quarters of the audience did not agree with me—neither did the host or producer.

I admitted that it would be *better* (the key word being *better*) for just one of two people having sex to get AIDS, rather than both of them getting the disease. It would also be better for a teen to have drugs at home, with a good needle and a paramedic on hand, than to go into the streets. And I said that if someone were going to jump off a bridge to commit suicide, it would be better and less painful to get him a gun!

"But better and best and right and wrong are two different things," I pointed out.

"Don't tell us what is right and wrong. Those are rights for you and not for us," a woman cried out. She claimed that 80 percent of all teens are sexually active. Although I know many teens have sex on a regular basis, I do not believe it is 80 percent—it's probably more like 40 percent. No one knows for sure the exact percentage. Here's how they inflate the figure: They include married teens and teens who have had sex once or twice and deeply regret it. (These teens are called secondary virgins—they are saving themselves from here on out for marriage.) The reason Planned Parenthood and other groups use inflated figures is to support their contention that abortions and condoms should be available to teens. I suggested that Faith Daniels survey the teens in the audience, but she didn't want to embarrass the hundred or so teens there.

During a commercial break, I heard the producer tell the host I had gotten in too much time. They did not want to hear any more conservative ideas, and they would not call on any more of the guests who supported virginity before marriage.

I burst into speech when the last segment started and warned the man who allowed his daughter to have sex at home that he was starting a dangerous precedent. "How much is enough?" I asked. "What if five guys wanted to have sex with her in one night? Would you stop it?"

The host lost it and began to attack me personally. "What about you? Were you a virgin when you got married?"

"No," I said, "I wasn't. That gives me the right to talk about the pains and hurts sex outside marriage causes. I can tell people how it almost ruined my marriage. Nothing good will come out of having premarital sex."

After those statements, I knew I'd never be asked back. I knew I did not have the agreement of most of my peers at that station—or in the television audience. But I also knew that not telling the truth hurts teens and parents. It can scar lives and destroy families.

I'm glad I stood up against teen sex. For a few minutes I had an unpleasant time, but some people heard that it is wrong to have sex before they marry—and I hope they took it to heart.

I must admit, it wasn't easy to go against all those people when I made my stand for what I deeply believe to be right and in the best interest of all concerned. I've learned over the years, after making many wrong decisions (and a few right ones) that pleasing people isn't as important to me as doing what God wants me to do. It's never comfortable and seldom convenient to stand up and go against the flow, but it sure does make you feel great inside. I have to live with myself, not the rest of the world.

You see, I enjoyed the price I paid in the loss of popularity at NBC. My picture would never hang on their walls along with those of hundreds of stars that have been on one of their shows. I felt good inside. The feeling of integrity filled my very being. Some people say I paid the price to be on that show. I say you pay the price for using drugs, breaking the law, cheating, getting pregnant, and dying from AIDS. Paying the price and enjoying the price are two different things. If you stand up for yourself—understanding who you are and what you believe in—you too can enjoy the price.

All your life you will contend with peer pressure. Though you may never appear on television, you will encounter people and situations that force you to make decisions. When you face the temptation to give in to the boy who wants to have sex with you, the friend who offers you a joint, or the co-worker who encourages dishonesty, you need strength to do the right thing. Wise choices don't occur when you give in to the whim of the moment—or the heavy pressure of someone who does not have your best interests in mind.

Whether you give in or STAND UP to peer pressure, you will pay a price. The right decisions will cost you in the short run—you may experience anger, ridicule, even hatred. But these decisions will help you for the rest of your life. The wrong ones will taste sweet at first but make you pay bitterly in the end.

I know you can make good choices, even when the pressure is on. You just have to be prepared for the pressure and know what to do about it. *Stand Up* provides you with concepts that will help you make good decisions for the rest of your life. It will show you how to identify peer pressure, evaluate what its results will be in your life, and decide what to do about it.

You've got a great future ahead of you, so STAND UP for yourself.

The Ups and Downs
of Peer Pressure

What does the term *peer pressure* mean to you? Are you thinking about the day you went out with a friend and did something you're sorry for but would never admit to anyone? Or has it become a comfortable excuse for doing what you wanted to do anyway?

Take the Peer Pressure Identification Quiz to help you decide how you would define peer pressure.

Peer Pressure Identification Quiz

When do you feel peer pressure? Put a check next to the items on the following list that best describe peer pressure situations to you.

Peer pressure is:

- ❑ When classmates tell me I should agree to have booze at the dance because everyone else drinks

- ❑ When friends laugh at me because I don't agree to go to the mall

- ❑ When I know I should help a sick neighbor and my friends encourage me to do it

- ❑ When I tell my best friend he's a dweeb if he doesn't want to go to a violent movie

- ❑ When I hear teens attack others but don't feel I can stand up for them, because I fear what others will say

- ❑ When I decide not to cheat on a test because I know my friends will be disappointed in me

- ❑ When I pick up a salad for lunch but put it back when my best friend asks why I'm eating "rabbit food"

- ❑ When my friends and I stand up against a guy who's giving girls a hard time and tell him to beat it

- ❑ When I start hanging out with people who get good grades, because I want to learn how to do better in school

When you hear about students getting drunk, girls getting pregnant, or a student who does poorly in school, people often blame it on peer pressure. When I ask teens about peer pressure, they can always give me a long list of negative things it caused them to do. But everything on the quiz above described the influence one person had on another—*that's* peer pressure.

Peer pressure doesn't always make you do bad things. If you get in with a positive crowd, it can help you improve. It can encourage you to:

Try out for a play
Eat better food and stay in shape
Say no to drugs
Decide to go to a better college
Study harder
Memorize Scripture
Start a new club

It can challenge you to do your best in a tough situation or help you make small decisions—like choosing what you want for lunch.

Peer pressure doesn't always make you do bad things. It can help you improve!

Which Peer Pressure?

Peer pressure comes in three varieties.

Helpful pressure. This kind encourages you to do something positive for yourself or others. When you go out for the team, become the leader you could be, finish a project, or help another student because a friend encourages you to, peer pressure works for you.

Harmful pressure. When someone tries to coerce you to drink, lie, steal, have sex, or do anything that could hurt you, it is harmful pressure, and you need to avoid it. Sometimes that will include avoiding the person who does the pressuring.

Ho-hum pressure. When you are urged to choose a Big Mac over a double cheeseburger, try out for the play instead of the chorus, or buy a red shirt instead of a green one, your choice is unlikely to strongly influence your life. Because these are only short-term decisions with short-term effects, this everyday pressure doesn't mean much.

Now that you know about the three kinds of peer pressure, read the following examples that will help you tell the three apart.

Good Pressure and Bad Pressure

Read each of the following stories. As you go, identify the kinds of peer pressure you see in each. (There may be more than one kind.) Then ask yourself: Who is pressuring whom? Why is the pressuring taking place? How would I respond in this situation?

In his freshman year Alan joined the band so he could learn to play his trumpet better. At first he didn't feel as if he fit in, but after a few months he'd become good friends with Tim and Lisa, and he looked forward to practice. The three of them would get together after school to jam, and he started to really improve musically.

In the summer before his junior year, Alan's mom died, and he felt so sad that he didn't even want to pick up his horn. When Tim asked him over to jam, Alan made excuses. Only when band started in September did he begin to play again. Then he practiced furiously.

When it came time to choose a horn player for a solo part, the band leader chose Lisa.

"I guess I'll just quit band," Alan told Tim. "I really messed up when I tried out for that solo. Maybe I'm no good at all."

There are three kinds of peer pressure: helpful, harmful, and ho-hum.

"You had a rough summer, Alan," Tim comforted him. "Give yourself a break! Once you start practicing consistently, you'll get better again. Just give it time."

Alan thought about that advice and made a habit of practicing daily. In his senior year, he was chosen to do the trumpet solo.

Bernice had a lot of fun going to the church youth group. She had never gone to a church with so many teens, and something always seemed to be going on—concerts, games, and meetings were only part of the youth group plans.

Barry also came to the youth group meetings. He seemed really interested in what Pastor Jensen had to say and asked a lot of good questions. He and Bernice started dating, and they talked a lot about God.

After a few months Barry began to push Bernice to have sex with him. Bernice felt as if she'd have to choose between Barry and her friendship with God and other Christians. When she thought about it, she preferred her friendships in the youth group to dating Barry. So Bernice turned him down flat. "Before I knew God, I might have gone along with you. But now I know I'm worth more than that. If you want to date me, you have to go by God's rules," she told him.

Barry dated Bernice a few more times, on her terms, then started seeing another girl. He never showed up at church anymore and lost interest in God.

"If you don't drink, you can't be part of our crowd anymore," Ted jeered at Ricky. "We don't want to hang around with wimps like you!"

Ricky looked at the faces around him. No one else in his circle of friends said a word—not even Jose, his best friend. So he grabbed the bottle Ted offered and took a few mouthfuls.

Why do people do this? Ricky wondered as he tasted it. It burned in his throat unpleasantly. But he didn't say a word. *Maybe I'll get used to it,* he thought.

Later Jose told Ricky, "I'm glad you did what Ted said. If you hadn't, we couldn't be best friends. After all, if you're not part of the group, we can't spend much time together."

Though he didn't like drinking, Ricky kept it up. After all, he needed friends, didn't he?

"What do you mean, you've never had sex with anyone?" Vonda could hardly believe what she'd heard. "Nancy, this is the nineties. No one believes in 'saving herself for marriage' anymore. Why, everyone else I know is having sex. Are you weird or something?"

Nancy felt hurt at her friend's comments. *Was* she weird? The next day she talked to her friend Kay. "Nah, don't even listen to her," Kay advised. "I know lots of kids who won't have sex. They just don't advertise it. You do what's right, not what Vonda says."

Nancy felt better knowing she was not abnormal. After that she and Vonda didn't spend much time together, but Nancy decided it might be better that way.

Often the pressure we feel is from within.

"Check out this dress." Rhonda took it off the rack to show it to Evelyn. "That shade of blue goes great with your eyes! You'll look awesome!"

Evelyn held the dress up to her and shook her head. "I don't know, Rhonda. I really like the red one over there."

"So try them both on," Rhonda suggested. "But I think you'll like the blue better."

In the dressing room, Evelyn saw what Rhonda meant. The red was too strong for her soft coloring, but the blue looked just right. She really would look awesome at the dance next week.

"Thanks, Rhonda," she said as she paid the cashier. "You really know what looks good, and I'm glad we went shopping today."

When Todd got into the car, he always put on his seat belt. At first Maria didn't feel as if she needed one, but when she noticed Todd's habit, she started to feel funny about not using hers. After a while she buckled up whenever she and Todd went anywhere.

One day Todd told Maria that his good friend Andy had been killed in a car accident. "The ambulance driver said his seat belt could have saved his life, but Andy

During the first part of my life when I was living for myself, before I knew Jesus Christ as my Lord and Savior, nine out of ten times my peers influenced me negatively. They had no more wisdom than I did. They had no more purpose in life or reason for doing the right thing than I did. They were lost, and so was I. In the past fourteen years, since I've been walking with the Lord and choosing to identify with people who have similar beliefs and values, I have been encouraged by my peers to do such things as write books, hand out my testimony pamphlet at high school assemblies, and go to Russia and hand out Bibles.

didn't have it fastened. If he hadn't been so proud about not using one, he'd be here today," Todd said.

Be honest with yourself. Look at where the pressure's coming from. Stand up for yourself!

That afternoon, as Maria got into her car, she fastened the seat belt. Somehow Andy's story made her feel afraid. What if that happened to her?

Did you identify positive pressure on Alan from Tim, on Barry from Bernice, on Nancy from Kay, and on Maria from Todd? Negative pressure was put on Bernice by Barry, on Ricky by Ted and Jose, and on Nancy by Vonda. Rhonda put some ho-hum pressure on her friend Evelyn.

The people we see every day have a lot to do with how we act. We want people to like us, admire us, or do things with us, so we often follow along and do what they suggest—even when we never would have done it on our own. You might say none of us lives in a social vacuum. No one is a rock or an island.

If a friend's opinion causes you to take on a new challenge, help someone, or start a good habit, the pressure works for you. If you are pushed into doing less than your best in school, attacking other people, or becoming addicted to something, peer pressure has harmed your life.

Everyone's life is influenced by other people. That's why it's important to know who will hurt you and who can help you.

In the next chapter we'll look at the people who pressure us.

CHECKPOINTS ✔

Review or discuss the chapter using these questions.

1. Name some peer pressure situations you have been in. Who put the pressure on you? What were you expected to do? How did you react?

   _____

   _____

   _____

2. Define what peer pressure meant to you before you read this chapter. What does it mean to you now?

_____

_____

_____

3. Name the three kinds of peer pressure. Describe situations you have been in that have involved each.

_____

_____

_____

4. When you look back at your life, have your peers helped you more than they have hurt you, or hurt you more than they have helped?

_____

_____

_____

The *Peer* in Peer Pressure

P eers are the people around you, usually those about your age, who share something with you. Maybe it's a friend who goes to the same school, a teen you know from church, or a buddy on a sports team. You often act the same, share the same interests, and think alike.

Because you have a place, activity, or attribute in common, when you have different thoughts or ways of doing things, you can feel pressure to act or think in the same way he or she does. Maybe your peer gives you a funny look when you say something, disagrees with you politely, or tells you straight out that you are wrong. Anyway, the pressure mounts for you to conform.

When people pressure you, they have one of two motives: They care about you deeply and want to see the best in your life, or they don't care about you at all but don't want to feel *they* are doing the wrong thing, or they have something to gain (either profit or pleasure) if you act in a certain way.

When the pressure is on, you may find it hard to tell the first group from the second one. You can do it if you keep in mind the following people pressure guidelines.

Positive pressure comes from people who:

- Have your best interests at heart
- You can be proud of
- Will support you until the day you die, even if you lose touch with them
- Want you to be happy and have peace in the future
- Have cared about you, shed tears over you, and prayed for you
- Love you deeply

Negative pressure comes from people who:

- Don't really care about you
- Care about themselves more than you
- Want the best for themselves, even if it will hurt you
- Want to avoid the guilt you make them feel when you say no

- Need company in their bad choices because they don't want to be alone

- May profit from your bad decisions (for example, companies profit when you smoke or drink, using their products).

Positive People

When people influence you for good, you can usually pick them out by their selfless attitudes. They think about your needs and best interests. Who are some of these special folks?

God. He created you in his image. He loves you and made you different from anyone else in the world. Instead of intending that you thoughtlessly go along with the crowd, he gave you the ability to choose.

If God had wanted robots, he could have created them. Because he wanted us to choose to love him, he gave us the ability to tell right from wrong. Every day, choose to put yourself in his loving arms. He wants to be your loving Friend, your Lord, and your Savior. If you don't already know him, accept his forgiveness for your wrongs and take the salvation he offers. It's the best choice in the world.

Positive pressure will come from people who love you and want what's best for you.

Parents. Unless you are in a home filled with physical, emotional, or sexual abuse—or other deep problems that can hurt a home—your parents love you and want the best for your life. Although they may not always understand how they can best help you, know exactly what to say, or approve of all your friends, they care about you more than anyone except God. For thousands of hours they have loved you, worried about you, provided for you, and otherwise looked out for you. They have changed your diapers, dried your tears, prayed for you, agonized when your friends hurt you, debated over what they should buy you, and felt sorry when they could not spend time with you.

Sure, your parents have made mistakes. Your dad might not have made it to the big game, and your mom might have put you off when you wanted to share your biggest problem with her, but occasional lapses don't mean they don't care.

Other relatives. People in your immediate and your extended family truly care about you. Your grandparents, aunts and uncles, cousins—and yes, even your brothers and sisters—usually have your best interests at heart. You may fight with a cousin or wish your brother or sister would go home and stop bothering you, but when a crunch comes, they will be on your side more than the casual acquaintance who tempts you to make a mistake.

Special teachers. Some teachers have the ability to see your potential, give you a helping hand, and care about your future. Though they have nothing to gain from you, they want the best for you. Also include your pastor, youth pastor, and other youth leaders in this group.

My little girl Emily has a special Sunday school teacher. Last week, for my daughter's birthday, Mrs. Ingram took Emily to her house for dinner. Emily became the Ingrams' guest of honor for that day. During the Chinese dinner, everyone had lots of laughs. Then Emily and her teacher baked some of the best-looking peanut-butter-and-chocolate drop cookies I have ever seen. Mrs. Ingram had nothing to gain by

---

The qualities we should look for in others are inside things— honesty, integrity, caring for others, being able to say "I'm sorry."

---

giving up her evening, yet she gave Emily a wonderful experience.

Friends. Some friends your own age have their heads on straight. Because they feel good about themselves, they don't need to prove themselves to other people. When you compliment them, they accept your words. When they see you making a mistake, they warn you ahead of time. Sometimes you can be serious with them, and other times you lighten up. They make the right choices in their own lives, and they want the same for you.

The problem is that usually these people don't belong to the "in" crowd. You may not feel as if you are part of the action when you spend time with good friends like these. The temptation to move with a fast crowd that makes bad decisions may be strong.

Identify the people who want the best for you by comparing them to the Supporters Checklist. When someone has most or all of the qualities on this list, you can count on their having a positive influence on your life.

Supporters Checklist

A supporter:

- Has your best interests at heart
- Wants you to have the best life possible
- Never lies to you
- Doesn't encourage you to break the law
- Would not want you to do something you would be ashamed of later
- Encourages you to plan for the future
- Wants you to be successful
- Helps you develop your skills to their fullest
- Has no ulterior motives

Compare your friends, family, and other special people to this list to discover your loving supporters. List their names and the help they have given in the Supporters Guide.

Supporters Guide

Write down the special people in your life who have given you help, encouraged you, or guided you to do your best. Describe how they have influenced you and think of a way you can tell them how much they have meant to you.

	Name	Influence	My Response
1.			
2.			
3.			
4.			
5.			
6.			
7.			
8.			
9.			
10.			

Plan ways in which you can make your supporters a stronger part of your life. Do you need to spend more time with them, do something for them, or come up with a creative idea to let them know you care?

Stop right now and fill in the spaces above with the "life-touchers" God has placed in your life. This is one time you don't have to stand up. You can sit down, but start writing!

Negative People

Be thankful for the good people who have helped you reach where you are today. But realize that not everyone you know will have a positive impact on your future. There are people, including some you have never met, who try to sway you into making bad decisions, following their way, and harming your own life.

Advertisers. Many teens never think about the influence advertising has on their lives. When they go along with the ideas they see on TV and in the media, they don't stop to think about the motives of the advertisers.

Teens who "go for the gusto" because a TV ad shows people drinking and having fun are missing the hard truth: Alcohol is the number-one killer of teens. Naturally the beer company will never advertise that fact—it would harm their sales, which would cut back on their profit. Advertisers want money from teens. The glamorous life they show on the screen has nothing to do with reality. Beer will *never* get you the woman you could love for a lifetime, success on the sports field, or a better job.

Its the same with the tobacco companies. Though the government makes them place a warning on the side of each package, they make it as small as possible. Instead of telling you about the risks of cancer, heart disease, and other health problems, they show a cute cartoon figure aimed to appeal to young people. They want you to become addicted and spend your money on their product.

Addictive substance users. Anyone who pushes addictive substances on you does not have a positive influence on your life. Drug pushers want your money, not a bright future for you. The kid who drinks at a party, and encourages you to drink too, does not think about the harm he might cause you. Though he may not gain money, he wants your company. When a "friend" joins in, the wrongdoer doesn't feel so wrong or so alone.

Sex pushers. When a boy wants you to have sex with him, what do you have to gain? To lose? Premarital sex will not improve your life or make your future happier. What it may do is give you a sexually transmitted disease or make you pregnant.

Does the boy who pressures you to have sex have your best interests in mind? NO! He may want some fun tonight, but he doesn't care about the pain you'll feel tomorrow. If you came to him and told him you were pregnant, chances are that he'd be history, even if you've dated him a long time.

Ask Magic Johnson if the women who went to bed with him were thinking about his best interests. Ask anyone with AIDS if she wishes she'd done some things differently. Plenty of people who used to be sexually active are stopping because they've been warned about the dangers of sex outside marriage. They've asked themselves this question: Is it worth ending my life early for a short time of pleasure? I don't think so.

Manipulative friends. Do you have a friend you just can't seem to do without? Even though he or she makes you do things you'd be ashamed to tell your parents about, you feel as if you'd fall to pieces without that friend. A friend like this should be on your negative list. He or she is not your best friend because he is trying to gain from you. That friend may be gaining momentary pleasure by convincing you to have sex. Or a friend like this may feel power when you agree to steal or cheat with him or her. What your friend gains, however, becomes loss for both of you. It will never contribute to your success in life.

Identify the damaging friendships in your life. People who want to own your time, make you lie, steal, cheat, and so on will not improve your life. Either you need to have more control of these friendships, so you can do the right things, or you need to make new friends.

Community manipulators. Anyone who is only out for your money and does not have your best interests in mind earns a place on your negative list. Include the people who run pornography shops here. They don't care about the sexual addiction or the danger of child abuse that could result from it. They just look for your money. When Hugh Hefner started *Playboy* magazine, he did it for the cash, not as a favor to the community. Don't believe anyone who does something harmful to mankind.

How can you identify the people who do not have your best interests at heart? Compare them to the Negative Influences Checklist.

Negative Influences Checklist

A negative person or organization:

- Never seems to make the right choices
- Often gets into trouble and expects others to bail him out
- Depends on you because you always make better decisions
- Seems to care for teens but has a lot to gain from them
- Encourages teens to have sex, drink, or use drugs
- Gives you the feeling, deep down, that something is wrong
- Expects you to do something illegal

Once you've identified the people who could harm your life, take action.

Perhaps you can help a negative friend turn his life around through counseling, support, or life-style changes. If not, you may need to spend less time with him and make new friends.

You can avoid being swayed by advertisers when you ignore the ads, walk out of the room when they are on, or turn off the TV set.

Once you decide not to drink, you need to stick with your decision by stopping your contact with parties that serve alcohol.

Negative Influences Guide

Use the Negative Influences Guide to identify people and groups who have caused or could cause trouble in your life. Then decide what you need to do about each relationship or situation.

Person or Group   Harmful Situation   My Response

1. _____
2. _____
3. _____
4. _____
5. _____
6. _____
7. _____
8. _____
9. _____
10. _____

Making Your Future Brighter

Recently I spoke with an old high school friend. At forty-one, Larry is just getting out of jail. He's been in and out of prison since I've known him, because he always seems to make the wrong decision. Never has Larry been able to see himself as a winner, and it is easy for him to feel sorry for himself and continue down the wrong path.

In contrast, my friend Steve has had a positive influence on my life. Though he has never done anything that made the news, at forty-one he has a beautiful family, a nice home, a prestigious job, and a wonderful marriage. He coaches his son's Little League team and has taught his kids right from wrong.

While Larry has a pity party, Steve has great peace and can sleep at night because he likes who he is.

The opposite attitudes of these two men were apparent even when I knew them in high school. Larry always made wrong choices, and Steve made the right ones. Larry tried to push the edge and dare the system;

Your friends *will* influence you, so choose friends who share your beliefs and ideals.

he always did small, destructive things. Steve taught me how to draw the line.

In high school I did not know Jesus as my Savior. Because of that, alcohol and marijuana nearly ruined my life. My abuses nearly cost me every friend I had; later they did cost me my house, my business, and my chance to father children. The drugs left me sterile, and the depression they caused almost cost me my life.

As I look back on my friendships, I can see why some of my old friends have gone down the road I started on and some have gone on to better lives. A few of my friends are not alive today because they made wrong choices. Those wrong choices, combined with the wrong people, backfired. My friends did not live to tell about it.

I don't want to see you end up like Larry, with a life full of bad decisions that have blasted your future. But I know that unless you put a lot of positive people and good decisions into your life now, you could experience a lot of heartache and pain as a result of the things you do today.

If you haven't filled out the charts in this chapter, take some time to complete them. Identify the people who can help you make the most of your life. Then we'll look at ways you can develop some positive plans that will help you reach good goals. Once you've stopped blaming peer pressure for your poor decision making and exchanged it for a positive method of planning, you can take hold of life in new ways and see many of your dreams come true. And remember—the reason you're going through all this effort is because you're worth it. So stand up for yourself!

I can't blame the negative people in my life for all my mistakes. I chose to do what I chose to do. I have to accept the responsibility for it.

CHECKPOINTS ✔

Review or discuss the chapter, using these questions.

1. What causes the pressure you feel in peer pressure?

_____

_____

_____

2. Name the different kinds of motives that can lie behind peer pressure. Describe each.

_____

_____

_____

3. Describe a positive person. What qualities does he or she have? How can you identify the positive people in your life?

_____

_____

_____

4. List five kinds of positive people you can have in your life. Do you have them in yours? Name them.

_____

_____

_____

5. Why are the supporters in your life special? Do you need more of them? How can you develop support in your life?

_____

_____

_____

6. Describe a negative person. What qualities does he or she have? How can you identify the negative people in your life?

_____

_____

_____

7. What damage have negative people caused in your life? How can you avoid their influence?

_____

_____

_____

Making Your Mind Matter

ou looked up at his English teacher in surprise. "You want *me* to enter the writing contest, Mr. Coleman? How could I do that? You know I only make Bs in class!"

"But you're still one of my most creative students, Lou. Your story lines are always imaginative. If you worked on your grammar, used a dictionary, and typed your papers more carefully, you could ace this course.

"Besides, you'd have three months to prepare. You could write a rough draft and go over it a couple of times. I would help you with your mistakes and give you some writing tips."

Lou liked the idea, but he just shook his head. "Nah, I've never done anything like that before. I'm just not good enough. Besides, my friends would think I was a nerd."

Is Lou making a decision based on peer pressure? Not really. Though he used his friends as an excuse not to enter the contest, his choice has a lot more to do with what he thinks about himself than what others think of him. He's afraid of both failing in the contest and looking bad to other people.

No one placed a gun to Lou's head and insisted that he avoid writing. In fact no one said a word to him against it. The "peer pressure" that made him avoid something he'd have liked to try was all in his own head.

Most of us have good imaginations when it comes to peer pressure. We can predict what others will say about our actions and "just know" what is and isn't cool. Without a word, we defeat ourselves, tear down our ambitions, and avoid things we didn't want to do anyway. None of this has to do with what others think about us; it simply reflects what we think of ourselves deep inside.

The Pressure from Within

Much of the time when we blame peer pressure for an unwise decision we've made, it wasn't direct peer pressure at all. No one tried to change our minds, but we looked at the situation, guessed at the popular opinion, and acted accordingly.

"No one ever told me I had to have sex with Russ," Leanne admitted. "Later I found out that most of my friends didn't approve of what I'd done. But television, the radio, and the people in the school health clinic

What you have on the inside determines how you respond when you feel pressure to do something you don't agree with.

always seem to think it's the natural thing, and I didn't want to be unnatural anymore. If I'd known then what I know now, I never would have done it."

Leanne could have stood up to the pressure. After all, it didn't even come from her friends. She wasn't that serious with Russ and didn't feel as if she couldn't say no. But media and other people had made her curious and doubtful of herself. The pressure came more from inside herself than from an outside source.

Leanne isn't the only girl who had sex because she didn't want to think others didn't approve of her, only to find that she'd lost the approval of the people who mattered most in her life. But unlike many teens, Leanne isn't trying to place the blame for her decision on the people who influenced her. "I made a bad choice," she says. "*I* made the choice, not the people on the radio, the school nurse, or anyone else. I can't change what happened with Russ, but I can make certain it never happens again.

"I made this decision because I believed the wrong people. But worse than that, I doubted myself, or I would have said no when Russ wanted to do what I knew was wrong. Today I'm building on a better foundation—one that says I'm of value, just as I am. The people I listened to didn't care about me. Today I know who does love me and where to go for good advice."

Unlike Lou, Leanne has learned to take responsibility for her own choices. She knows that a lot of this mental pressure doesn't come from the outside, but from the inside.

A girl assumed from hearing her classmates talk that she was the only one in her class who had not had sex. She was humiliated and didn't want to be different from everyone else, so she decided to do something about it. There was a boy who was known to have had sex with many girls, so on a cold night, she went with him under the bleachers of the football stadium and had sex. It quickly got around school. It also got back to her that many of the other girls had been lying and had not had sex before.

People seldom think the things about us that we expect they will. They're probably not thinking about us at all! Stand up and follow your heart.

What you have on the inside determines how you respond when you feel you aren't part of the "in" group or you don't agree with your friends. It gives you either the strength to say no or the go-with-the-flow attitude that leads to unwise yeses.

Fighting Back against Peer Pressure

When you don't think much of yourself, you can put yourself down, as Lou did, or you can just follow "cool" people because you think they are more important than you are. Either way, you put yourself in a dangerous position—you look to someone else to make choices for you, even if they aren't the things you'd really like to do.

In order to withstand the peer pressure that your mind conjures up—or the real peer pressure that comes when others try to put you down, change your mind, or influence you—you need to know who you are, why you are valuable, and how you can relate well to others. With this knowledge on the inside, you can make better choices on the outside.

Who Am I?

You don't have to be in this world long before people start letting you know what they think of you. Maybe your family has always compared you to your sister, put you down, or abused you. If so, you will have been bombarded by the message that you aren't much at all. If your family and friends have usually supported you, encouraged you, and shown you how to do better, you will have a good opinion of yourself.

All of us have some idea of who we are, where we want to go in life, and what we need to do. But we also know of ways in which we have messed up, missed out, or avoided doing right. No one is perfect, but the good news is that we are improvable models—we don't have to stay in the same place we're in today. To discover ways in which you can improve your self-esteem, read my book *Stand Tall*. There you'll find practical advice that will give you a new understanding of the things that have made you special and those that have torn you down.

Before you can spread good emotions to others, you need to love yourself. When you believe that you have no worth, you do anything to seek a friend's approval. That's why looking at yourself first is so important.

Why Do I Have Value?

Do you know that there is no one just like you in the whole world? The next time someone wants you to go along with the crowd, think about that and know that you have your own individual personality, needs, and future. You don't have to go along with another person's decision unless you know that it is right and good for you.

God made each one of us with our own gifts, abilities, and personalities. To him, each one of these attributes is special, and he wants us to make the most of all he has given us. When we know we have value in his eyes, the opinions of others become less crucial in our decision making. Instead of going along with the crowd, he gives us power to stand up for him and make the right choice.

Putting People in Their Proper Place

You have value to other people, too. Your mom and dad, brothers and sisters, and good friends do not use you for their own ends. They love you because they know you, care for you, and want the best for you. Do

God gave you a place on this planet, gifts to offer the world, and a reason for living.

you value them enough? Have you tried to build good, strong relationships with them by developing communication lines, spending time with them, and sharing your life with them? The people who love you most should be part of your inside stuff, but they won't be if you close them out.

Other people are important, and I'm not trying to encourage you to forget them, ignore them, or hurt them. But until you can see yourself as a special person who has value, you are likely to let others lead you into bad choices or take over your life.

You have a place on this planet, gifts to offer the world, and a reason for living. Though you should treat others with respect and love, do not wipe out your own importance by assuming they will always know what is best for you.

Instead, turn to God, who can help you balance the other people in your life with your own worth. He can show you when you need to avoid negative people or help them turn over a new leaf. He can show you how to improve relationships with friends, your family, and other important folks in your life.

When you have God's values in your life, you will know when to give in to pressure that could help you and when to turn from what could harm you. As you grow in him, the good choices will come more easily and naturally.

Dealing with Mental Pressure

When you think about what others will say of your actions, is it ever positive? Do you imagine other people saying:

"Did you hear about the good job Ethel did as a hospital volunteer?"

"James is a good student because he studies so hard."

"I sure appreciate the way Valerie helped me with my homework."

"If I could be like anyone I know, it would be Mike."

Probably not. So often in mental peer pressure we imagine that others will put us down, think the worst, or not like us. How often do we think they'll say:

"Only geeks go to church."

"You'll never pass that test."

"Why do you spend so much time studying, Four Eyes?"

"No one wants to take you to the prom because your nose is too big."

"I don't want her as my friend."

Have friends actually said these things to you? Sure, once or twice you might have gotten into a fight with someone who really let you have it: "I wouldn't sit next to you in class if it were the last seat in the room and my grade depended on it." Maybe you caught her on a bad day. But more often the put-downs that live inside your mind didn't really start with someone else. You have taken your own habitually negative thoughts and placed them in other people's mouths.

How can you take control of your put-down thinking? Take the following steps.

Let Go!

Perhaps you remember a time when someone said:

"You are a loser. I don't know why I put up with you."

"Your brother always gets As. What's wrong with you?"

"Who would be friends with you?"

"Why don't you listen?"

People in your past have told you such things, and you've hung on to them, repeating them in your own mind. Instead of letting go of the hurt and forgiving the person who said the words, you've accepted them as being true.

Before you can lose these voices, you'll need to evaluate them. Was the friend who said, "Who would be friends with you?" jealous, hurt, or in a bad mood that day? Did your mom say, "Why don't you listen?" when she was frazzled from a hundred chores she couldn't complete? Perhaps the words weren't an accurate evaluation of your total life. Realize that, and do not allow those words to ruin your value in your own eyes.

If you got straight Ds in your freshman year but your sophomore year saw you earning As and Bs, don't let the comparison to your brother's grades fester. You've made changes and improved your life. Let the comments go.

Sometimes people say things that hurt, and we can't change the situation. Maybe their words have a grain of truth in them, and we can't avoid that. Then the only answer is to forgive. Unless we can put destructive statements behind us, we will carry them for the rest of our lives.

Once we let negative words run through our minds, they often seem to expand. Pretty soon, it's not just the words someone actually said that put us down, but all the other imaginary conversations we can invent. Before long we are negative people who say negative things about others, too. No wonder people don't rush to be our friends.

"I used to always criticize people," Anna told me. "It wasn't that I meant to hurt people—I honestly thought I was helping them do better. But I didn't have a lot of friends. One day at church Sally talked to me about the way encouragement works." Anna smiled. "That one little lesson changed my life. She encouraged me, and I started to feel good about myself. Then I wanted to pass that on to others.

"You see, when you criticize people, it doesn't make them want to do the right thing; it just puts up all their defenses. But when you tell them what they have done right, they want to do better.

"Now I always make certain I say nice things to people. When I have ideas for them, I say them in the kindest way I can and let them take hold of the idea in their own way."

Her smile grew wider. "I have lots of friends now—and they're much better than the ones I had before. All it took was a change of attitude."

When no one encourages you and you come down on yourself all the time, you can't say much that's positive. So start today to live around positive people, to forget to jump on yourself when you make a mistake, and to forgive others when they mess up. As positive ideas fill your heart, you'll pass them on to others.

Change Your Focus

Focusing on the good in life, accepting that people can love you even if you are not perfect, and living for what is right will help change those negative voices that whisper reminders of how you've failed. Daily you will need to choose not to believe the worst about yourself, turn to God for forgiveness when you've done

---

As you grow in God, the good choices will come more easily and naturally.

---

wrong, and decide to do the right thing. It may not come naturally at first, but soon you will find it second nature to see things from a brighter perspective.

When trouble comes into your life, start saying things like:

"I love God, and I know he's with me in this."
"Lots of people care about me, even when life isn't going my way."

"I can make it through this—lots of other people have."

"The good decisions I make today will help me later."

"This won't last forever—good choices will."

Though you may not feel as if you are a great success, hold on in faith that you can make it and do the right thing for today. You may not see results for a while, but in the end you'll be happy with your decisions.

At first the negative ideas you've lived with will come back often. Just don't accept their truth—fight back! The struggles you face will be worth it.

Derek's dad would never win an award for father of the year. Every time his son made a mistake, he came down hard on him. "I remember hearing that I couldn't do anything right from the time I was little," Derek told me. "By the time I was fifteen, I didn't even try anymore. It seemed to me that if my dad couldn't believe I had a chance, no one else would either. I was really headed down the tubes.

"Then I met Mr. Johnson. For the first time I had someone who thought I could do things right. When he found out I liked sports, he helped me join a baseball team and even made sure I got to practices. For once I heard 'You can do it, Derek,' instead of 'You can't do anything, Derek.' It make a big change in my life."

Today Derek has a lot to hope for. Not only did his success in sports help him physically and emotionally, he's begun to improve in his schoolwork. "My guidance counselor thinks I have a chance at making it into college, even though my freshman grades weren't all that good. He's given me something to work for, and I'm trying hard."

Derek has had to learn that his dad's view of his life is not the only one. People who believe in him have given him new ideas.

"But most of all, I've been able to say to myself, *Look what I can do!* When my mind tries to tell me I can't win, I have ammunition against it. I remember Mr. Johnson and my guidance counselor, too. If they can believe in me, I can believe in myself.

"I'll always love my dad," Derek said sadly. "But he has had a tough life. Because of his struggles, he had a hard time feeling good about people, even his family.

"I've learned that people can throw garbage at me, but I'm the one who chooses to live in it. When I say no, I put the garbage where it belongs—in the garbage can."

Learn from Mistakes

But what if you have really blown it? Maybe you have made unwise choices: started smoking, and now you have an addiction; treated people badly, so they don't want to be your friends; or had sex before marriage. How can you feel good about yourself again?

Use these steps to start yourself on a new path:

1. Identify what you have done wrong. This is very important. Be specific. Have you made a bad choice, hurt someone, or broken God's laws? Face up to the truth squarely.
2. Pray, asking God's forgiveness. Make it right with him first.
3. If possible, make amends. Ask for forgiveness. Apologize to the person you hurt, pay back the person you stole from, or do whatever you can to make things right. Sometimes it's better not

to go to the person you've wronged. For example, if the person isn't aware of what you've done, it may just hurt him to bring it up.

4. Forgive yourself for your mistake. No one is perfect, and allowing the mistake to hang over you means you do not really accept God's forgiveness. Consciously accept his forgiveness on a daily basis until you really believe in it.

5. Learn from your mistakes. The only positive result of making mistakes is learning what you should avoid, how you can do things better, and how to help other people in need. Make this error a springboard to better things, not a swamp to wallow in.

What needs to change in your life? Write it down, commit yourself to change, and begin today.

Building a better self-image may take time and effort, but in the end it will give you the ability to stand up against peer pressure, reach goals in your life, and aim for a future you can look forward to.

CHECKPOINTS ✔

Review or discuss this chapter using the following questions.

1. Was Lou's decision not to enter the writing contest based on peer pressure? If not, what was it based on?

   _____

   _____

   _____

2. Have you made decisions based on what other people might think about you? Did they think the way you expected? Describe the situation.

   _____

   _____

   _____

3. When you make choices based on what others might think, are you making a choice based on peer pressure? Why or why not?

_____

_____

_____

4. What is the real basis of mental peer pressure?

_____

_____

_____

5. Why is mental peer pressure negative? Name three ways you can combat negative mental pressure.

_____

_____

_____

6. How can you turn negative thoughts to positive ones? Outline a plan of attack.

_____

_____

_____

7. Have you learned from your mistakes in the past? How have they caused you to change your life? How has that benefited you?

_____

_____

_____

The Harm in Following the Crowd

Harmful peer pressure is very real. You feel it every day when someone gives you messages like these:

- Prove you really love me by having sex with me—I'm using protection.
- To be in with the "right" crowd you have to do drugs.
- Cheating is okay. After all, even the teachers expect it.
- Getting good grades means you are a Goody Two-Shoes.
- Spending time with your family is dumb. They aren't important.

- No one likes teachers. They just don't count.
- Cool people don't ask questions in class.
- God is boring. The Bible is archaic. Don't be old-fashioned by believing that stuff.

The list could go on and on.

Whenever you do something wrong or don't do something good because you are afraid of what others will think or do, you are a victim of negative peer pressure. What others think has made you captive to their ideas, unable to think for yourself and seek the best goals in your life.

What Price Are You Paying?

Most people assume you have to give in to negative pressure in order to be "normal." I disagree. So often I've seen teens who gave in to the pressures of so-called friends—and paid the price. Look at some of the hurt peer pressure can cause.

Being part of the crowd will never make you a leader in your school, a person people remember with pride, or a success in the future.

- Chet didn't want his friends to think he was too smart, so he didn't do his best on tests. When it came time to apply to college, he couldn't make it into the school of his choice.
- Kyle stole a ten-dollar cassette and landed himself in the juvenile home for a year and a half.
- Richard got drunk at a party. His friends told him to have sex with a girl at the party. Today she's pregnant with his child, and he hardly even knows her.
- Sharon didn't even like booze. Her parents were alcoholics, and she knew where drinking could lead. But when her friends wanted to drink at a party, she went along with it. Every time she drinks now she does something stupid and hurts someone.
- Marcy is only eighteen and has had two abortions. Now she has nightmares and can't forget how she took the lives of her babies. When she gave in to her boyfriends' pressure to abort the children, she never knew about the pain she'd feel today.

Being part of the crowd will never make you a leader in your school, a person people remember with pride, or a success in the future. It could cause you a lot of heartache and leave you with many regrets. That's why I want to give you some tools that will help you identify negative pressure and avoid its consequences.

Your Negative Pressure Toolbox

When you face a decision and need to know if you are looking at negative pressure, ask yourself the following six questions:

1. Is it based on truth? So much peer pressure is based on lies or false assumptions. People get abortions because they believe that the child is just a "mass of tissue," not a real human being. Girls have sex because they confuse lust and excited hormones with love.

But the truth will not cause you harm in the long run. It will not sway you to make a decision that will bring you pain forever, and it will not distort what is real.

When you don't follow the crowd, you can often be sure you are following the truth. Going the opposite way of most people might make you a leader. When you live up to what is right, honest, and good, you will feel positive about yourself.

2. Would I do this if my parents or God were here? The truth is that God is with you all the time. But if you knew your parents could see you right now, would you do this thing? Would you drink that? Would you go to this place? If the answer is no, you can be sure you are making a poor decision.

Feeling bad about what you do is very healthy. It can keep you from doing wrong or repeating a mistake. Make use of this warning system in your life.

3. Do I feel good about myself after I do this? All the time I hear from teens how awful they feel after they've had sex and their boyfriends are gone. How terrible they feel after they've used the drugs or drunk the booze.

Minimize regrets in your life by not repeating the mistakes that cause them. If it's wrong, don't do it.

4. Would I want this activity written up in the news-paper? If everyone could read about what you've done, would you feel good—or miserable? Answering this question truthfully could eliminate many things from your plans.

While you try new things and seek excitement, be careful that you will not regret your fun. Don't do wrong just because it is popular and common. You are too special to make that mistake.

5. *Does this activity show true concern for others?* Selfish activities will not make you a better person. Anyone who wants to take, take, take shows little concern for you and will not improve your life. You do not need such friends. Avoid people who want to date you so they can have sex—they're more likely to give you AIDS. In your own actions make certain you help others, reach out to hurting people, and think how what you say could hurt or help them.

6. *Would my future be better if I did this?* When I speak at schools, I ask teens to name someone who used alcohol and improved his life from that use. No one has given me a good answer for my question. Alcohol has never bettered a person. It only tears down dreams,

I have poured my life into this book and I want you to find the truth about your life through it. Please don't take the easy road out. Walk the path that is seldom walked—the one that has brush on it and that few people go down. It is a narrow path, but it is exciting and wonderful, as well as tough. You have to stand up in order to see over the branches and see that there is a light at the end of this path. Though few will travel it, you can be one of those few.

Write the five questions below on a 3 x 5 card and put it where you'll see it every day.

futures, families, and hopes. It only makes people worse. Drinking can never brighten your future.

Then I ask teens to name someone whose premarital or extramarital sex has improved his or her life. No one can give me an answer for that either.

When you have asked these questions, you can also ask yourself, *What are the consequences of this for me?*

Could this activity kill me?
Could it ruin my dreams?
Could it tarnish my feelings about myself?
Could I lose the respect of others?
Could I hurt my reputation?

If you answered yes to any of those questions, the activity is not worth it. Though you may avoid paying the price in the short run, you are going to pay in the future. It ain't over till it's over. When you know a super stud who has sex with every girl he can get his hands on, you may not know he has AIDS—until ten years later. (And if he doesn't get AIDS he'll be haunted by the memories of all his past sex partners every time he has sex with his wife.) Someone who speeds may not get caught, but one day he may lose his life in an accident, or spend his life in a nursing home because doctors can't fix the damage the accident did to his body. Look beyond the fun today to the future you have tomorrow.

Don't Be Part of the Problem

You have felt the sting of negative pressure. People have tried to make you do things their way, go along with what's wrong to make them feel right, or follow their leadership when they didn't have our best interests at heart. But maybe you have also led others to do wrong by pressuring them.

"I really messed up!" Len admitted. "Just after I met John, I insisted that my friend Tom hang around with him, too. John was new to our school, and I thought he needed friends.

"After a few days, Tom pointed out that John wasn't very honest. When our math teacher gave a quiz, John hadn't studied, so he wanted to see Tom's answers before he handed in his paper. I thought it would only happen once, and I told Tom not to make too much of it.

"Tom didn't say a lot about John after that. They weren't close. But when we went out, the three of us usually went together.

Peer pressure isn't just what happens to *you*—you may do it every day to others.

"Tom's brother Stu came with us a few times. He and John really hit it off. Until later I didn't find out that there was a lot more about John that I didn't know. He was involved with a car-theft ring, and he was looking for more kids to get involved. From the start he'd known that Tom and I wouldn't go for it, but he knew he could meet people through us.

"Stu got involved in the ring and got into a lot of trouble. How I wish I'd listened to Tom and never insisted that they stay friends!"

Pressuring people can lead to plenty of trouble. Len didn't intend to hurt anyone—he only wanted to help a new teen in his school. But in his "love me, love my friend" attitude toward Tom, he was exerting peer pressure on his friend.

Peer pressure isn't just what happens to *you*—you may do it every day to others, too. How do you feel in the following circumstances?

In a conversation, people do not see things your way.

You and your friends don't dress in the same styles.

Your friends go places with people who aren't your friends.

Your group doesn't get involved in all your after-school activities.

Do any of these situations make you feel uncomfortable? When you feel this way, what do you do? Do you push your best friend to join your team, even when he doesn't want to? Do you make fun of someone who doesn't wear the latest fashions? If so, you are pressuring them to do things your way.

Everyone pressures other people at some time. Often it's a passive pressure to agree, join in, and have fun. Sometimes we get mad when others don't do things our way or see eye to eye with us. As much as possible, we need to understand that people are individuals. We should be sensitive to our friends' needs to do things their own way, get involved in ideas and activities that can help them for the future, and become the best people they can be.

As long as your friends are moving forward, doing the things that will improve their futures, don't pressure them to follow your path. It's when you see them making mistakes that can hurt their lives that you need to lovingly confront them and gently pressure them to do the good things that will build their lives.

Remember, the people who pressure you can have your good at heart. Make the pressure you put on others' lives the kind they will thank you for in the end. Stand up for others because they are worth it, too.

"Later I found out that Tom stuck with me because he did not want John to hurt my life," Len shared. "When I found that out, I felt so humbled. Tom and I are working now to help Stu out of his trouble. I feel as if it's my fault he met John, and I want to help him find better friends."

CHECKPOINTS ✔

Review or discuss this chapter using the following questions.

1. What is negative peer pressure?

   _____

   _____

   _____

2. What are some questions you can ask yourself when you face negative pressure? Which ones would be most effective for you?

   _____

   _____

   _____

3. What five questions will help you identify the consequences of giving in to a specific pressure?

   _____

   _____

   _____

4. How have you exerted negative peer pressure
   on someone? What was the result?

   _____

   _____

   _____

Taking the Harm out of Peer Pressure

P eer pressure can hurt, but it doesn't have to. That's why I want to share this simple, four-step strategy that will help take the sting out of it. The strategy is summed up by four words:

> Perception
> Planning
> People
> Purpose

With these, you can chart a course that will avoid the rocks that other people, your own lack of under-

Are you seeing yourself and others clearly or does peer pressure cloud your vision?

standing, or your own wrong choices could be putting in the way of a successful voyage through life.

Perception

Each of us sees things differently. Our perception is our reality.

"I thought it would all turn out right," Mary cried to me during a counseling session after I had spent two days at her large high school. "I thought he loved me, and I believed he had my best interests at heart. When he said that someday we would marry and it was okay to have sex now, I accepted that. He said I'd never regret it, but I *do*." The tears streamed down her face.

Mary thought she'd made the right decision. David, her boyfriend, had seemed like a caring person who would always look out for her, but now that her senior year was ending, Mary discovered he wouldn't be part of her future. Where had she gone wrong?

Mary had the wrong perception of the situation. She saw sex as being okay—in the circumstances. The problem was that the circumstances changed. Although David seemed to care about her, once she had sex with him, their relationship lost the challenge he needed. He saw her as conquered, and he looked for someone new to attack.

How we perceive things has a lot to do with how we act. I have met convicts who told me they never thought they would get caught, and some who had convinced themselves they'd done nothing wrong. Their ideas could not have been more mistaken—and prison came as a great shock to them.

How do you perceive yourself and others? The answer to that question will influence your choices. Are you seeing clearly, or does peer pressure cloud your vision?

Do you fear what other people might say about you or do to you, if you don't follow the popular idea of the moment? That negative perception will not lead to what's best for you. Do you have to agree with your friends in order to have stature? Then you'll go along with others because you want to feel good about yourself. But following the crowd will not give you the results you expect. Do you do it because you think others will admire you? If so, you are wrong! No one looks up to a follower who never makes his own choices. Making your own decisions, based on clear thinking, will gain you much more admiration.

When you look at yourself, do you see a special, valued person? Unless you envision yourself that way, you will not avoid the things that destroy you.

"I can't have that attitude," Doug objected. "It makes me sound as if I thought I was better than anyone else, and Jesus said we were to be humble."

I'm not suggesting that you get a swelled head, just that you know the worth God sees in you. You don't have to go around bragging about your talents. Doug's wrong, because valuing yourself, one of God's greatest creations, has nothing to do with pride or humility. It's simply believing that God made each of us a loving, caring, awesome person. He makes no mistakes!

To understand yourself, you need to know what God says about you. Take a look at these key truths in verses that describe you from his point of view.

1. You are made in God's image. From the moment he made you, he had a lot in mind. That's why he made you like him.

> Then God said, "Let us make a man—someone like ourselves, to be the master of all life upon the earth and in the skies and in the seas."
>
> [Gen. 1:26]

2. You are just below the angels. If you see what angels are like in the Bible, this has to amaze you. God says you are important—just a level below these supernatural beings!

> When I look up into the night skies and see the work of your fingers–the moon and the stars you have made— I cannot understand how you can bother with mere puny man, to pay any attention to him! And yet you have made him only a little lower than the angels, and placed a crown of glory and honor upon his head.
>
> [Ps. 8:3–5]

3. God knows everything that goes on in your life and cares for it. You are so important to God that he keeps track of every little detail in your life.

> And he knows the number of hairs on your head! Never fear, you are far more valuable to him than a whole flock of sparrows.
>
> [Luke 12:7]

4. God loved you enough to give up his own Son for you. How many of us could give up a much-loved child for someone else? That's what God has done for you. He gave up what he cared for most so that he could have you for eternity.

> For God loved the world so much that he gave his only Son so that anyone who believes in him shall not perish but have eternal life.
>
> [John 3:16]

5. Nothing in this life can keep his love from you. No matter what troubles you must face, God will never leave you.

God loves me, even when I goof up over and over again.

> For I am convinced that nothing can ever separate us from his love. Death can't, and life can't. The angels won't, and all the powers of hell itself cannot keep God's love away. Our fears for today, our worries about tomorrow, or where we are—high above the sky, or in the deepest ocean—nothing will ever be able to separate us from the love of God demonstrated by our Lord Jesus Christ when he died for us.
>
> [Rom. 8:38–39]

6. God enables you to love others the way he loved you. You can begin to love other people in a selfless way.

You won't even want to do wrong when you realize how much God loves you and gave for you and how much you owe him.

> If you love your neighbor as much as you love yourself you will not want to harm or cheat him, or kill him or steal from him. And you won't sin with his wife or want what is his, or do anything else the Ten Commandments say is wrong. All ten are wrapped up in this one, to love your neighbor as you love yourself.
>
> [Rom. 13:9]

Though Satan would love to destroy you, when you perceive yourself as a deserving person—only because of God's love—he cannot do it. See yourself through God's eyes every day.

So step one of the process is to see yourself and situations that you are in through God's eyes.

Planning

Step two is making a plan that will help you make the right choices. Failure to plan leads to failure.

Whenever I talk to teens in trouble, over and over again I learn that they made the same mistake: They never had a plan. They didn't know where they were going, so they followed the crowd. At the last moment, they always agreed to do what others wanted, even if

Failure to plan leads to failure.

they didn't know what would happen. In the end, they were sorry—after it was too late.

One stupid party ruined Jim's entire sophomore year—and may influence his whole life. He got drunk, and when someone offered him marijuana, it sounded like a good idea.

"Until we got caught, that is," he admitted. "I got kicked off the team, and it ruined my chance at college. I'd wanted a sports scholarship, but that one night probably ruined it. It didn't make any difference that I'd never used drugs before—they caught me in the act."

Today Jim knows that he could have avoided that mistake by having a plan not to go to parties where there were drugs and booze. "Tell other teens how important it is to think ahead," he said, "so they don't end up in my position."

The basic steps for making a plan are:

Step 1: Try to verbalize the types of peer pressure you might encounter. Write down the things that concern you, being as specific as possible.

Step 2: Think about all the possible ways you could respond to the pressures.

Step 3: Discuss these answers with someone you respect (usually someone older and wiser).

Step 4: Decide on the best response for each pressure and commit yourself to it.

Step 5: Talk to one or two good friends who will support you in your commitment.

Step 6: Ask for God's help in keeping your commitment.

Without a plan, you could end up in Jim's shoes. But with one that identifies trouble spots, you can skirt a lot of problems in life. The next two chapters will help you develop positive plans that can impact your life—and the lives of others.

People

The next step is choosing to be around people who will not hinder your effort to make good choices.

How do you choose the people you want to hang around? Perhaps you look for the coolest crowd in school or date the guys who most annoy your parents. Remember, you usually become like the people who have the most influence on you: friends, family, and co-workers. Chances are also very good that they will influence you more than you will influence them. This is especially true when you become part of a crowd.

Recently Susan shared her story with me. "When I joined the drama club, I thought I could have a real impact on what was going on. Even though I knew they were hard on people, I thought my faith as a Christian would touch them.

"I wish it had worked that way. At first people listened to me. They seemed interested in God. But after a while, they realized I wanted them to believe, and they didn't want to do that. I became odd man out. The members of the club ignored me or teased me about my faith whenever I mentioned it.

"I didn't mind not being Miss Popularity, but I couldn't influence people in the cast when they wouldn't even listen.

"Gail, another student, joined partway through the year at the suggestion of our advisor. She seemed okay to me, but the president of the drama club, Sean, made it clear that he wanted her out—he called her a spy. He passed the word that everyone should tease her until she went away. I knew it was wrong, but by then I was really caught up in working on the play's scenery. I couldn't quit and let everyone down, so I went along with the crowd by not doing anything.

"One day when I left school I found Gail crying in the auditorium. Sean had given her a hard time until she just couldn't stand it.

"I remembered what trouble I'd had when I shared my faith and felt bad that I'd done nothing to help Gail. Then I realized that ever since they teased me, I hadn't been a good witness for Christ. I'd lost sight of my real goal and had even begun to do what they wanted. The crowd told me what to do, and I never really thought about how it might hurt Gail."

People can make you do things you'd never think of doing otherwise, distract you so that you make mistakes, and make you doubt your values.

That's why parents and teens often disagree about friends. Mom and Dad may want you to spend time with someone you can't stand, but they object to your best friend. Why? Because they want the best for you, and they know that if you're not careful, you could be influenced in harmful ways. When you bring home friends, your parents can usually tell when they are trouble. Because they have experience with people, they can see when a girlfriend is spoiled and wants her own way, or when a boyfriend will try to push you around. Parents can often spot character problems that teens miss. So ask your parents what they think and take their advice when they see trouble ahead. It could save you a lot of pain.

People have an important role in helping you avoid negative peer pressure and making good decisions. We've already identified the positive and negative people in your life. Chapters eight and nine will help you harness positive pressure and make it work for you.

Purpose

Do you have a purpose in life, or are you just wandering through? Plans help you with the day-to-day choices, but you need to develop a broader purpose, too. Where do you want to be five years from now, ten years from now, and at the end of your life? Who can help you get to your goal, and what action do you need to take today to get there?

You may not hit all your goals, but a larger purpose in life will keep you from sweating the small stuff and help you avoid a lot of problems.

Jeff was an honor-roll student in high school who wanted to become a doctor. "Sure, I could have gone to more parties, spent more time with friends, and gone to the shore more," he said. "But I knew that putting time into those and avoiding studying would never get me into a good college. If I didn't go to a top-notch college, I couldn't get into the best medical school. So I was willing to give up some weekend plans for my future.

"I just got accepted into an Ivy League school. If I keep my goals in sight, I can make my plans come true. Now all the parties I missed don't mean a thing."

Jeff has a goal that will take a lot of work, but he's also developing the self-control and study habits that can make him successful in his chosen field. Every step of the way is important, so today he's making the decisions that will help his career.

Perhaps you hate science and could never become a doctor. That doesn't mean you can't make decisions today that fulfill your purpose for tomorrow. You do it every time you:

- Say no to sex because your life and future marriage are too important to put at risk
- Avoid drugs because you only have one brain—and it needs to last a lifetime
- Choose after-school activities that will build your skills and help you learn teamwork
- Make friends you can be proud of
- Read your Bible so you can learn more about your eternal future
- Spend time with your family, even though peers tell you parents are uncool
- Challenge a friend who is stealing, because you care for his future more than you care what people will say
- Share the Gospel of Jesus Christ with someone who doesn't know him. You are doing something to help change another's eternity. You are pleasing the awesome God that loved us so much that he sent his one and only Son to die for us so we could live. When your purpose in life is more than just pleasing yourself you will be one of the most fulfilled people in the world. Being unselfish, thinking of others, and fulfilling God's plan for you is very satisfying.

Discover where you want to be in the future, and start planning for it today. This could change your entire life.

If you don't like what's happening in certain areas of your life, you need to make a plan and make some changes.

CHECKPOINTS ✔

Review or discuss this chapter using the following questions.

1. What is perception? How does it influence the decisions you make?

_____

_____

_____

2. What does God have to say about you? Why do you need to share his view of you?

_____

_____

_____

3. How does planning help you avoid mistakes? Make better decisions?

_____

_____

_____

4. How do people influence the choices you make? How do you decide what people you want to be with?

_____

_____

_____

5. What purpose do you have in life? Do you need to develop new goals and plans?

_____

_____

_____

Decisions, Decisions, Decisions

I only had a moment to decide," Fred commented. "The car would be left alone for a few minutes while the driver went inside a store. My buddies made it clear that I had to steal that Jeep or I wouldn't be part of their gang—ever.

"I sure am glad the cop car came around the corner at that moment. If it hadn't I might have given in and done something I would have regretted all my life. No friends are worth the trouble I would have gotten into with the legal system—and my parents."

Fred had his decision made for him when the police appeared, but most of us have to make split-second decisions without such intervention. Choices need to be made at inconvenient times, when we have lots on our minds.

Even if we make the right choice, that decision may be put to the test again and again. Perhaps we say no the first time a friend offers us drugs—but is it just as easy the second, third, and fourth times? When a date keeps pressuring for sex, does the heat turn up?

Planning for Good Decisions

Teen years bring a lot of tough decisions every day. You begin to discover truths about yourself and life, and the good and bad things they hold. But is knowing right from wrong enough?

Not unless you have a plan to put that knowledge into action. You may have to make the same decision over and over, until it seems dull, and you seem boring for saying no all the time. The gibes of others when you won't do drugs, have sex, or go places you know will get you into trouble can make you tired of being the party pooper. When you wonder if you've made the right choice, because you feel as if you're alone in the crowd, you need to know what you are fighting against; then you need a purpose and a plan to keep you on course.

Do you have a purpose in life? What is it? Check out the Life Purpose Quiz to identify where you are going.

Life Purpose Quiz

Which of these goals best describes what you want for your future?

- ❑ I want to have fun.
- ❑ I want to help other people find God. Maybe I'll be a pastor or a missionary.

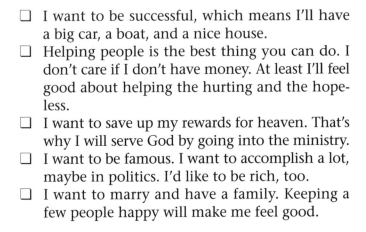

❑ I want to be successful, which means I'll have a big car, a boat, and a nice house.

❑ Helping people is the best thing you can do. I don't care if I don't have money. At least I'll feel good about helping the hurting and the hopeless.

❑ I want to save up my rewards for heaven. That's why I will serve God by going into the ministry.

❑ I want to be famous. I want to accomplish a lot, maybe in politics. I'd like to be rich, too.

❑ I want to marry and have a family. Keeping a few people happy will make me feel good.

The quiz is intended to make you think about what you want out of life and what goals you have. Evaluate your answers by asking yourself the following questions.

Did your life purpose focus on material possessions, yourself, or on helping others? Did your answers show that you want to follow God's plan for your life or were you only out for yourself?

Your attitude toward your goals reveals a lot about you. It can also give you an idea about how much you are influenced by your peers. People who focus on having things and good times usually give in easily when they know their popularity is at stake. There's very little they wouldn't do to look good. Standing up in an argument for someone who has been wronged or for an idea takes a lot of courage—and a purpose that goes beyond popularity.

If you have a purpose, you can stand up and choose the best for your life, whether it is politely telling a waitress your steak is not done correctly or saying to your girlfriend, "I respect you too much to give in to these sexual desires." Your enthusiasm for good choices will come from the heart; that means you'll be a person of integrity.

To be a person of integrity, you need a firm base for your life. Take the Integrity Test to see how you rate.

To be a person of integrity, you need a firm base for your life.

Integrity Test

Check the statements that best describe your reactions.

- ❑ 1. When I run into a rough spot, I try to be honest with other people, even if it will hurt me in the short run.
- ❑ 2. If the truth would hurt someone, I bend it a little. After all, I have to consider their feelings.
- ❑ 3. When I go to work, if I don't know what to do, I ask someone. It doesn't matter if a co-worker thinks I'm dumb as long as the job's done right.
- ❑ 4. If no one tells me what to do on the job, I just guess. If it's not done right, someone else will fix it later.
- ❑ 5. When I don't agree with my teacher, I meet with her after class so we can talk it out.

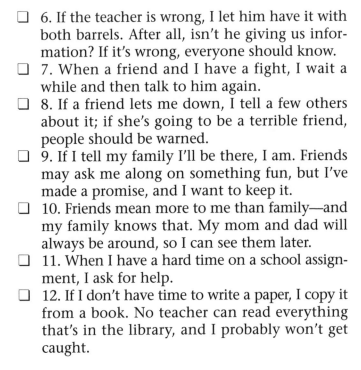

☐ 6. If the teacher is wrong, I let him have it with both barrels. After all, isn't he giving us information? If it's wrong, everyone should know.

☐ 7. When a friend and I have a fight, I wait a while and then talk to him again.

☐ 8. If a friend lets me down, I tell a few others about it; if she's going to be a terrible friend, people should be warned.

☐ 9. If I tell my family I'll be there, I am. Friends may ask me along on something fun, but I've made a promise, and I want to keep it.

☐ 10. Friends mean more to me than family—and my family knows that. My mom and dad will always be around, so I can see them later.

☐ 11. When I have a hard time on a school assignment, I ask for help.

☐ 12. If I don't have time to write a paper, I copy it from a book. No teacher can read everything that's in the library, and I probably won't get caught.

Now score your test by giving yourself a point for each odd-numbered statement you checked. How did you do?

5–6 *You have lots of integrity. It will serve you well.*

3–4 *Integrity may not be your middle name, but you have an idea of what's right and wrong. Discover ways to improve your stance and become the kind of person others look up to for your good character.*

1–2 *You need to take a look at the basis of your life, the way you treat others, and how you see right and wrong.*

Perhaps you got a good score on the Integrity Test—or maybe you bombed out entirely. Either way, you need to establish some guidelines for your life and decision making. Your daily life, the ideas that mean the most to you, the thoughts you give most time to, and your concepts about people will all feed naturally into the way you make decisions when life turns into a pressure cooker.

Perhaps you thought the Integrity Test was pretty easy. Well, how do you answer these questions?

1. Is there really a right and a wrong? Where does God say so?
2. Why should one person be honest if millions of others aren't? What difference will it make in the giant scheme of things?
3. If ten people are in a life raft and there isn't food or water enough for all of you, what should you do? Should you kill the elderly or the sick? What does God say about the greatest love?
4. Even though abortion is a legal right, is it right?
5. If right is right and wrong is wrong, will it ever be right to break the law or hurt someone?
6. Why are you able to have food, shelter, and Guess? jeans while millions of others don't even have enough to eat?
7. Does God really have a plan for your life? Is your future worth standing up for?
8. What would you die for? Your country? A child about to get hit by a car? Your freedom? Your beliefs?
9. What are you living for? What is your life all about? When people think of you, what comes to their minds?
10. Should a professional athlete be paid fifty times more than a nurse who cares for dying children?
11. What would make a person a good president of the USA?

Quickie Questions

"I hated drugs, because I had seen what they did to my brother," Alice said. "He lost touch with our family, dropped out of school, and ended up feeling sorry for himself, so I knew that drugs weren't fun. But I felt so lonely during my senior year, when my best friend moved away. Kelly seemed to have it all together; her life wasn't sad like mine. So when she offered me drugs, I decided to try them.

"What a big mistake that was! Right away I knew this wasn't for me, and I chose never to do it again. But I hate to think how easily I almost ended up like my brother.

"Drugs came into my life when I wasn't feeling good about myself. I was vulnerable, and it took no more than a suggestion to get me started. Today I encourage other teens to avoid drugs by knowing how to deal with problems creatively. You don't need drugs when you have a plan for your life, support from the people around you, and a deep faith."

When you face a major decision, how can you know that you're heading in the right direction? Do you have to take a survey of public opinion? Go to the library and find out what's current? Or ignore the question altogether?

No! Ask yourself the following six questions, and you will avoid a lot of trouble.

1. Does God say no? Today lots of people will tell you, "That's wrong for you, but it's right for me. After all, we live in a free country. I can do as I please." What they're really saying is there are no rules. Depending on the situation, you can do whatever seems right to you.

God's Book, the Bible, helps you know how life works best.

When people tell you to lie, cheat, or steal because it will be the "best" choice, don't fall into their trap. Nothing can make stealing right—it will only seem okay for a while. In the long run, you will pay the price for having taken what was not yours to start with.

You can't imagine playing Monopoly without any rules, can you? How would you know where to go on the board, whose turn was next, or when you'd won the game? Well, even more than the game company, God knows you need rules to show you what to do in life. So he's given you the Bible—his rule book that helps you know how life works best. He asks you to live by it, because life is happier that way.

You can choose to believe God, or you can go down your own path. He won't force you to follow him. But the direction he points you in will be better in the long run. By following his rules, you will avoid a lot of heartache.

When you need to make a decision, discover first what God has to say. Read your Bible, seek advice from your parents, pastor, youth leader, or Sunday school teacher, and ask yourself, *Does God say yes or no?* If he says no, avoid that action; when he says yes, make it part of your life. Remember, he didn't give you rules to hem you in, but to help you avoid the hurts of a mistake.

2. Does the law say it's wrong? Even though God's Word doesn't say anything about speeding, don't try to make a case for it in a court of law. When the policeman pulls you over to the side of the road, you've done wrong in God's eyes, too.

Though our government may not follow God in every way, he says he's given it to us for our good. That means you have to obey the laws it makes—unless they disagree with God's laws. For example, the Supreme Court will let you abort an unborn baby, and many Americans do. But God says we're living human beings even before we leave the womb. As a Christian, you need to do what's right, not what the law will allow. Murdering a fetus will always be wrong in God's eyes.

3. Will this hurt me in the long run? What if the law and God's Word don't tell you what to do? Remember this ditty: "If God's rules aren't black or white, will it lead toward wrong or right?"

For example, God's Word never mentions what to do on a date. But if you find yourself alone with your date in a parked car, you know your hormones could lead you to make some choices you'd soon regret. So bypass that parking space and drive on home, before you do something unwise. By avoiding putting your feet on the wrong path, you'll make a good decision.

When you see a gray path ahead, ask yourself, *What are my chances of going farther and regretting my actions?* Run away from the places and things that call you toward wrongdoing.

After all, if you only had a peashooter and you saw a Dodge City gunslinger walking the street calling your name, you'd disappear fast, wouldn't you? It's the same when poor choices stare you in the face.

4. Whom can I ask for advice? Some decisions call for help. When you can't see what's best, seek the advice of an older, wiser person who has your best interests at heart.

The latest song on the radio advises you to have a good time, and your friends may encourage you to do what it says. But you don't think that's the best road for you. Once you tell your buddies you don't agree, they start razzing you. "Hey, Preacher, no one does that nowadays. You'll be the only guy in this school who takes a girl home before midnight. What's so wrong with parking? It's never hurt me! I can't wait to tell the whole school this news." What do you do?

Parents, older friends, teachers you respect, or a minister or counselor may give you ideas that can help you stand up to the abuse.

Listen carefully to what they say and consider putting it into action. Maybe you'll need to do it in your own way, but you can take advantage of their knowledge and experience.

5. What are the long-term results? Many times we choose what looks good today only to find out that the results next year aren't quite what we expected. Sure, no one can see perfectly into the future, but we will avoid many problems if we keep an eye on what could happen down the road. Play-now-pay-later choices can often get weeded out at the start if we look to the future.

Spending your life as a single parent, living in poverty, or fighting an addiction for years need not happen if you plan today to succeed tomorrow.

6. What is my long-term plan? In the midst of an emotional situation, you can make bad spur-of-the-moment decisions. That's why it's important to plan ahead.

Sure, you can say no to premarital sex up to the last moment, but when you are half undressed on the couch, you may have trouble convincing your date you mean what you say. Better to avoid passionate situations than fight off a lot of hormones in a last-ditch effort.

Your best plan should include avoiding:

- Parties with drugs and alcohol
- Places where illegal or dangerous activities occur
- Premarital sex
- Pornography
- Stealing
- Cheating
- Putting yourself in ANY compromising position!

You can add to that list with specific things that tempt you but are not part of a long-term plan for good. Everyone has a few, and they're important to avoid ahead of time.

Make other people part of your planning by asking yourself, *Is this good for me and others?* Your future, your friends, and your family all deserve your best. Don't let your inconsiderate planning hurt others.

By asking yourself these six questions, you can avoid feeling embarrassed, dirty, or guilty. You can start developing your character, becoming a strong person who is not easily swayed by others. Today you can form habits that will help you for a lifetime—or you can head for the ones that cause heartbreak, misunderstandings, and depression.

Making It Real

Sure, it's easy to identify the questions to ask, but what does it take to put the answers into action? When it comes to doing the right thing, how can you make them work for you?

The people I associate with at my church and in my Bible study and my close friends influence me greatly. Our common bond is that we want to serve the Lord. We want to do what is right and oppose evil. Other people do not influence me very much because the more they tell me I shouldn't share my views and keep my religious beliefs to myself, the harder I try to be creative and tactful in doing what I know God wants me to do. Just because I receive opposition doesn't stop me. Jesus was crucified for the truth, so I can take a little heat myself.

When I surveyed over 7,500 teens across America, I discovered that over a third of them had been pressured to drink alcohol. Last week, at a party, Sam became one of those teens.

"I went to the next town with my best friend, Bobby," Sam explained. "We didn't know these people well—in fact, I had never met anyone at the party. Bobby had met our host, Kevin, once, and he seemed like a nice guy.

"When Kevin saw that we didn't have drinks, he came over and offered them to us. We said no, but asked if he had some Coke. He looked at us as if we were strange and said all his friends liked beer. I got a glass of water from the kitchen.

"All night Kevin seemed bothered by the fact that we didn't drink. He felt as if we couldn't be having a good time. He kept mentioning drinking until Bobby and I felt we were being really rude. About midnight Bobby gave in and took a beer. I told Kevin I was driving, and that stopped him from bothering me the rest of the night.

"I don't like feeling as if I have to choose between being rude and doing the right thing. When my friends and I go out, we need to know what to say. Can you help us?" Sam asked me.

I shared the six questions with Sam.

"If God says no, you don't want to do it. What does the Bible say about drinking? Look at what happened to some people who drank," I said. "In Genesis 9:20–27, look at Noah. He got drunk and lay naked in his tent. One of his sons started spreading the news, but the other two covered him with a robe. When Noah woke up, he felt embarrassed at what he had done and cursed his youngest son, who had told everyone.

"Then look at Esther 1:10–2:1. When the Persian king got drunk, he wanted his wife to parade before his drinking buddies. When she wouldn't, he banished her. Later he missed her, but he could not change the law he'd written, so he lost his wife."

Then I turned to Proverbs 23:29–35. "What does this say about drinking?" I asked. "What does it cause?"

"Pain and sorrow, fights, hallucinations . . ." Sam shuddered. "I don't need that in my life."

"Proverbs 20:1 says it gives false courage. It hurts lives and people. In Proverbs 31:2–9, God warns the king not to drink, so he won't forget his job.

"Do you need any more proof on what the Bible has to say?"

Sam didn't.

"The next question asked if it was legal. How old are you?"

"Seventeen."

"What is the legal drinking age in your state?"

"Twenty-one."

"Then the law says it is illegal for you to drink. God does not want you to break laws that are good for you."

Sam knew God didn't approve of drinking. Now he knew the American legal system didn't advocate it for him either.

"Now, will it hurt you in the long run?"

"I've seen what it does to people," Sam admitted. "I have a friend whose dad is an alcoholic. I sure don't want to be like him."

I asked Sam if he knew any way in which alcohol could help his life. He couldn't think of one, in the long term.

"You've already asked my advice. But you can also look at the statistics. Alcohol is the number-one killer of teens. It causes family abuse, rapes, suicides, and other illegal acts. The next time someone offers you a drink, remember that—and tell him, if you can."

"All of the long-term results are bad," Sam admitted when we came to the next question. "I can't see why people get started if these things could happen to them."

"Do your long-term plans include abuse, hurting others, and death?" I asked.

Sam shook his head.

"Then what good reason would you have to drink today?"

Sam began to realize that his future was more important than the pressure he would feel at the next party.

Happy is the man who doesn't give in and do wrong when he is tempted, for afterwards he will get as his reward the crown of life that God has promised those who love him.

[James 1:12]

CHECKPOINTS ✔

Review or discuss this chapter using the following questions.

The Bible teaches that all of our actions have consequences. Be careful what you choose.

1. What is your life purpose? How much is it influenced by your peers, parents, and others?

    _____

    _____

    _____

2. Do you have a lot of integrity? How do you know? If you need improvement, what can you do?

    _____

    _____

    _____

3. How does what God says relate to decision making? Do you use him as a resource? How?

    _____

    _____

    _____

4. What do you do when the law says something is wrong? When God says it's wrong? What do you do if they disagree?

    _____

    _____

    _____

5. Name ways you can identify decisions that may hurt your life. Who can help you figure out which decisions could hurt you in the long run?

_____

_____

_____

6. What good decisions do you need to make today? How can you make them part of your lifestyle?

_____

_____

_____

Does God Care about My Choices?

Does God really care about whether I go to the prom, buy a Toyota, or go out for the team?" Alex wanted to know. "After all, Bible times were so different from today, and I can't find anything in the Scriptures that talks about those things."

Alex was smart to realize the difference between Bible times and now. When the Scriptures were written, dating didn't exist. Rush-hour traffic consisted of chariot wheels and whips, not tires and horns, and most people walked to work. No one went out for football, because it hadn't been invented yet. But God hasn't left us up in the air. He may not mention culture, new inventions, or the latest craze, but he has given us principles to guide us in every situation. With his help we can make good decisions.

How can you do this? Look to the wisest source for your answers: God's Word. Based on what it says, I challenge you to make four basic decisions that will help you in all you do for the rest of your life.

1. Decide to love Jesus Christ above everything else. I encourage you to put him first in your life—above anything and everything, even your family.

> If you love your father and mother more than you love me, you are not worthy of being mine; or if you love your son or daughter more than me, you are not worthy of being mine. If you refuse to take up your cross and follow me, you are not worthy of being mine. If you cling to your life, you will lose it; but if you give it up for me, you will save it.
>
> [Matt. 10:37–39]

Knowing God this way gives you a "heart condition." By that I don't mean that your life is in danger and you need to see a doctor, but that you will be sensitive to what God wants you to do, and you will try to live out

---

Knowing God gives you a "heart condition"—you will be sensitive to what God wants you to do.

---

his will day by day. This will enable you to say no to the wrong stuff and yes to the good things for your life.

Loving Jesus isn't a one-time choice, it's a life style. With every decision you make, you develop new habits or build on old ones. That's why what you decide today may be important to the rest of your life.

2. Decide to pray before making decisions. Even Jesus, God's Son, prayed before he acted. He wanted to feel God's total calling and have peace in his heart, knowing he had done the right thing. Jesus wasn't interested in doing the easiest thing, taking the convenient path, or deciding what would be most fun. When you don't know where to turn in life, you can look to God for the answers. He will show you the way.

> If you want to know what God wants you to do, ask him, and he will gladly tell you, for he is always ready to give a bountiful supply of wisdom to all who ask him; he will not resent it.
>
> [James 1:5]

All you have to do is ask, and God is happy to answer. But don't expect to hear him shouting through the clouds. Though he could do that, more often he speaks to your heart in a still, small voice. When you are too busy going to the wrong place with your friends, you won't hear what he has to say. But when you stay close to him and pray often for his wisdom, you'll get used to hearing him.

Walk daily with God. Keep him on your heart, and he will help you avoid life-harming decisions. Don't only look for God in the huge revivals that reach thousands of people. He wants to be close to you, and his still, small voice can have all the impact it needs to have on your life.

When you live as a Christian should, you can count on one thing: You will be different from the crowd.

3. Decide to live God's way no matter what. Live for God because it is right and because it makes you feel good about yourself.

When you live as a Christian should, you can count on one thing: You will be different from the crowd. Often you will not make the choice that is most popular, but you will make the right one. Living for God will make you an immovable person of integrity, honesty, love, and gentleness.

Living all-out for God won't mean things will always go your way. It hasn't for others, and it won't work that way for you. Just read Hebrews 11 to see what happened to the heroes of the faith. Some of God's promises to them weren't fulfilled until they got to heaven, yet they trusted God and went on living for him. That's what he expects of you, too.

4. Decide to see the larger plan in your life. How did these great men of the faith manage to keep their eyes on God? They knew where their real home was and what was in store for them there.

These men of faith I have mentioned died without ever receiving all that God had promised them; but they saw it all awaiting them on ahead and were glad, for they agreed that this earth was not their real home but that they were just strangers visiting down here. And quite obviously when they talked like that, they were looking forward to their real home in heaven. If they had wanted to, they could have gone back to the good things of this world. But they didn't want to. They were living for heaven. And now God is not ashamed to be called their God, for he has made a heavenly city for them.

[Hebrews 11:13–16]

Make your faith in God the basis of your decision making. It will give you the ability to make wiser, better choices in your life. Decisions you make with God's help will not only benefit you—they will also serve him and touch the world forever.

We must walk our talk and be fed by the Lord day by day if we are to grow.

CHECKPOINTS ✔

Review or discuss the chapter using the following questions.

1. Does God care about your daily choices? How do you know?

   _____

   _____

   _____

2. Read Hebrews 11. What promises didn't the heroes of the faith receive immediately? What *did* they get?

   _____

   _____

   _____

3. How can you walk with God today? Name some specific choices you need to make that will help you do this.

   _____

   _____

   _____

What Fruit's in Your Orchard?

Have you ever tried to spend a day away from people? Maybe you were having a rough time and wanted to get off by yourself to think. Perhaps you felt as if you needed some space.

It wasn't easy, was it? Perhaps you closed yourself into your room. Just as you began to feel peaceful, your mom needed you to do a chore, a friend called on the phone, or your sister banged on your door. Getting people out of your life isn't easy.

Most of us don't want to avoid people for more than a short time while we're trying to work through some problems. Not having others to share with, learn from, and spend time with gets pretty lonely. When people avoid others for long spells, it's often a sign of emotional trouble in their lives.

Needing other people isn't weak or silly. God made us to be social—to help others and be helped by them. But the people we live with rub off on us a lot. When we're only with people who want to spend lots of money and own lots of things, we become like that. Soon we have a problem with greed—and we may wonder how we got that way. But if our friends think people are more important than things, work at building good relationships, and like to help others, we are likely to share similar goals and, therefore, have a well-balanced life.

We've already looked at the need to build relationships with others who have your best interests at heart. How can you spot them? It isn't always easy, but there are some important clues to watch for. You can tell a lot if you look at two key parts of their lives: the inside and the outside.

Inside Stuff

What is a friend like on the inside, where no one can see? The answer to that question will show you a lot about the real person you're dealing with.

Lots of people try to hide their true natures—and may even do it successfully for a while. "When I started dating Gary," Laurie told me, "he seemed like a really up-front guy. I thought he shared everything with me and was totally honest with people.

"One day he had an accident on his motorcycle. He was afraid of the heat his parents would give him for it, so he ran away from the site of the accident and lied to his dad about the damage to his bike. 'What he doesn't know won't hurt him,' Gary told me.

"When I threatened to tell his parents what had happened, Gary became nasty. 'You do that, and I'll never date you again,' he said. We'd been seeing each other

God made us social beings. Needing other people isn't weak or silly.

for a year, and we had become really close. I didn't want to give that up, and I certainly didn't want to be a tattletale, so I kept my mouth shut.

"As time went on, I noticed that Gary wasn't as honest as I'd thought. Soon I learned he had lied to me, 'for my own good.'

"But it wasn't good," Laurie admitted. "I broke up with him, and am I ever glad I did. Once I wasn't seeing him anymore, my friends started telling me a lot of things I'd never known about our relationship—and none of them were positive."

What Laurie didn't know about Gary's inside stuff could have seriously damaged her life. If they had married, his dishonesty could have led to divorce.

Look at the attitudes a person has about honesty, cheating, and relationships with others. Does she put people before her own gain, or is she out for number one and willing to do almost anything to get what she wants? Even someone who seems to have his life together may see nothing wrong with taking money under the table or lying to the people who love him. Though his life may be smooth today, he's heading for trouble tomorrow—and so will you if you follow his example.

Best Friend Quiz

If you had to choose a brand-new best friend or date, how would you want him or her to act? Check the descriptions of the people below who are most appealing.

- ❑ Don's younger brother needed help studying for a major math test. Don lent a hand, even though it meant he had to miss a game with some friends.
- ❑ When Rachel's mom's car broke down, Rachel couldn't take her to the garage. "Tom's going to pick me up in half an hour. What if we ran into traffic?" Though her mom pointed out that the garage was only five minutes away, Rachel still wouldn't budge.
- ❑ When a teacher told Anita she was too loud in class, Anita barked back, "What does it matter? No one learns anything in your class anyway!"
- ❑ Louise learned that Vicky was having a hard time in chemistry. She went to the teacher and asked if they could work in the lab after school so Vicky could catch up. Then she offered to tutor Vicky.
- ❑ "You owe me money," Rich bellowed at Marty. "Pay up or else!" Marty had borrowed the money to go to a movie with his girlfriend, Sue. *But if I pay him now, I won't have money to go out with the guys tonight,* Marty thought. "I don't have enough on me now," he lied. "I'll have it for you next week."
- ❑ When Arthur heard about the church collection for the homeless, he gave the ten dollars he'd

received as a birthday gift from his aunt. "It isn't much," he told the people who were collecting. "Maybe next month, after I've started my new job, I can give you more."

❑ Angela was offered a job after school. When it came time for her to get a paycheck, her boss just handed her cash. "I don't want anyone to know about this arrangement," he told her. "It's just between you and me." Angela realized he was not telling the government about her work. "I don't want to do anything illegal," she told her boss. "This will be my last day."

❑ Jules took Danielle out for a few months, then broke up with her to date another girl. Danielle had told him about many family problems. Now they were all over the school. When she confronted him, Jules said, "You never told me not to say anything."

Did you admire Don, Louise, Arthur, and Angela? They have the qualities that make good friends—friends who will help you and challenge you to achieve.

When you choose new friends, pick those who:

- Care for their own lives—who make it wonderful, exciting, and special to be around them.
- Respect other people. This shows they love themselves. As a result they can respect their parents, the law, teachers, and other people in authority.
- Listen well. People who can listen can communicate well. When you know what others think, you can understand them and respond to their needs.

These are friends you can learn from, grow with, and enjoy life with. You can share a lot with them, because they have the right stuff.

Fill in the chart using the names of two or three of your closest friends.

Friend #1		Friend #2		Friend #3		Tries to . . .
yes	no	yes	no	yes	no	
☐	☐	☐	☐	☐	☐	Treat others well
☐	☐	☐	☐	☐	☐	Help me think positively about myself
☐	☐	☐	☐	☐	☐	Listen carefully to others
☐	☐	☐	☐	☐	☐	Challenge me to do my best
☐	☐	☐	☐	☐	☐	Study hard
☐	☐	☐	☐	☐	☐	Listen to teachers and parents
☐	☐	☐	☐	☐	☐	Help others in need

If your friends do many of the things listed in the chart, you have made good choices. Encourage them to continue in this path.

But what if your friends aren't like that? What can you do?

Exchanging Old Friends for New

I won't tell you to start ignoring all your friends and meeting only new people, but I do want you to look at your friendships and turn them around if the negative outweighs the positive in your life.

I can honestly say that I have some friends I could call in the middle of the night for help. They would come to help me whenever I needed it and would take care of my family if they had to. We have strong, trusting relationships that have developed over the years.

Make your friendships growing ones, too. If you know someone who has trouble helping others, show him how to do it, and let him know you hope he will make it a habit in his life. Maybe his family has never learned the skills of caring for others, and your friendship can add to his life.

If you have a friend who is involved in drugs, let her know you care and will go with her if she seeks help. Commit yourself to spending time uplifting her, sharing with her, and making certain she has the resources that will help her turn her life around.

When a friend swears all the time, try to understand what makes her act this way. Does she do it because she feels bad about herself, thinks it's cool, or has fallen into the habit at home? Together work out a plan that will help her overcome her bad habit.

Do what you can to help a hurting friend, but don't destroy yourself emotionally if you don't always have the impact you would like. "When I found out Bill had a drinking problem, I told him I would help," Ray said. "But Bill couldn't see that anything was wrong. 'I only drink once in a while,' he objected. 'That doesn't mean I'm a drunk.' I shared some facts with him that should have helped him understand his problem, but he still would not admit that his drinking was hurting him. He would not seek help, even if I went to the counselor with him. What more can I do?" Ray wanted to know.

Ray and Bill aren't very close anymore. "I still see him once in a while," Ray said. "But I guess my confronting him made Bill uncomfortable. When I call he usually says he's going out with someone else or has a lot of homework.

"I pray for Bill all the time. Someday I hope he will look for help. If he needs me, I will be there."

Bill has to make the decision to fight his addiction. Ray can offer help, but he cannot make the choice.

Challenge your friends, help them; but if you need to move forward in a positive direction and your friend objects to your new life style, don't compromise your future for one friend—or even a group of them.

"When I became a Christian," Sue shared, "I lost all my old friends. The drug crowd I'd been hanging around started to call me 'Jesus freak,' and they didn't want to talk to me anymore.

"At first I felt really hurt," she admitted. "But pretty soon I understood why it had happened. God brought new friends into my life—people who could support me in my new faith and who lived without drugs, alcohol, or any of the other negatives in my old life.

"I've learned a lot from my new friends, and my life has turned around. Someday I want to have a positive influence on the friends who won't talk to me now. When they see where I have gone, I hope they'll know that they can do it too."

Trying to help friends can be a growth path for you, as long as you keep to God's rules. When you give someone a hand with what's on the inside and her life improves, other people will know it too.

Outward Actions

What you do and say results from the inside stuff— your ideas and beliefs. If a guy knows that honesty is important, he will treat other people honestly. If a girl has compassion for others, she will treat children, friends, and family well. A tree is known by its fruit; if you see apples hanging on it, you know it's an apple tree. When you see pears on the branches, you don't call it a cherry tree.

Just as you don't try to make cider from what grows on a cherry tree, you can't make people with bad actions positive, upstanding influences on your life.

Whether or not you know it, your life has an impact on others. Make it positive!

You can only encourage them to exchange their rotten fruit for the good kind.

When you look at what your friends do, what do you see? If your best friend is cute, and her looks have made her popular, realize she didn't do anything to gain that beauty. She may not have a strong character that will build a good life style. Before too long, you will be hurt and disappointed if you choose her as a friend only because of her outside stuff. Pretty people can make good friends—but only if they have the right inside stuff too.

Do you look for friends who have pride in themselves, who feel good about the way they live, the goals they have, and what they have accomplished, or do you look for the most popular people in your school, church, or community? Scoring the most points in a game, becoming prom queen, or going to the most parties does not make a person a hero. A hero is someone who has integrity and thinks of others.

What fruits do your friends bear? Do they build up others or tear them down? Do they make the most of their future or live only for today?

Get in with a crowd that grows lots of healthy fruit. In a few years you could own an orchard.

Cultivating the Fruit

The next time you hear about peer pressure having a terrible influence on someone, remind that person that people can have a positive impact as well. Then think of some people who encouraged you to get good grades, study hard, or use your mental abilities. Go thank that helper who improved your life.

Mitchell told me about his best friend, John. Without encouragement, Mitch would never have applied for seven or eight college scholarships. "It took extra work to do it," Mitch admitted. "But in the long run it was worth it. Two scholarships came through. That means that 80 percent of my tuition and all my room and board are paid for.

"Because of the financial help, my family will not have to scrimp and save as much in order to send my sister to college next year. That means a lot to me."

Mitchell isn't the only teen who thinks of—and acts for—others. In a small school I visited, a few teens wanted to meet to pray for their country and their school. They met around the flagpole in front of their school on planned days. Their numbers kept growing, and so did their prayers. Soon they were praying about their own lives, that they would reach the world.

Three teens from another school prayed throughout a week of assemblies that I gave with three of my friends, and we saw amazing results. Nearly one-quarter of the students stayed behind for counseling for their hurting lives—they wanted answers. One girl handed me a bottle of pills and told me my talk had kept her from committing suicide. The teens who prayed so hard did not even go to this school—in fact they came from another state! Their caring changed lives they'd never have touched otherwise.

After I spoke in another school, Susan and her best friend, Dana, came up to me and shared that they had just challenged each other to commit themselves to the best for their dating lives. Before they went on dates they planned to call each other up and encourage each other to hold on to their standards and live with integrity. Each would remind the other that God was with them on the date.

Susan and Dana wanted to have good fruit in their lives, and they were willing to help each other achieve that goal.

Live out your faith at home, at the mall, and on the way to school with your friends.

Actions God Loves

Jesus challenged the churchgoers of his day with the following words. As you read what he said, ask yourself if you are included.

> Jesus replied, "You bunch of hypocrites! Isaiah the prophet described you very well when he said, 'These people speak very prettily about the Lord but they have no love for him at all. Their worship is a farce, for they claim that God commands the people to obey their petty rules.' How right Isaiah was! For you ignore God's specific orders and substitute your own traditions. You are simply rejecting God's laws and trampling them under your feet for the sake of tradition."
>
> [Mark 7:6–9]

With these words, Jesus described people whose actions did not reflect their inside stuff. They liked to look good on the outside, but inside they faked it.

Jesus challenged his disciples and leaders to worship God with their whole hearts—not just when they were near the temple. In the same way, he does not want us to be "good Christians" at youth group and forget it when we go to school. Live out your faith at home, at the mall, and when you are driving to school with your friends. Don't limit his work in your life by only seeking him once a week. Every day live for him by choosing friends who will help you do your best. Then be a friend who encourages and challenges people to do their best for God.

A man named Chuck Holland encouraged me to stand up, put back my shoulders, and help other hurting students. "Every student in this college is going to get a sheepskin," Chuck told me. "That is what everyone is fighting for. They all want to graduate, and so do you. But you are going to do something extra: You are going to become a life toucher. You will notice people who are hurting and sitting alone in the cafeteria. You will notice body language and help students with their heads hung low. You will realize when someone needs a friend and you will become his friend."

Chuck's words helped me finish college and choose my career. He helped me learn what I pray you will learn from this book: Believe that you are special. Stand up for yourself. I'm thankful for the good things Chuck brought into my life by being an encouraging friend.

During a meeting on suicide, a boy stood up and told me about his friend Jim. "If it weren't for him, I'd be dead," this boy shared. "I attempted suicide twelve times, but no matter what I did, Jim stood by me. When I felt depressed, I called Jim, and because of his help I chose to live."

You are many people's peer, so become a positive-pressure one. Even when you don't realize it, you may be pressuring someone to do the right thing, live out his convictions, and improve his life. When you see a friend going wrong, you may help her make a better choice, reach out for God, and turn her life around.

Whether or not you seek to, your life will impact others. Make the best of it by always seeking to become a positive influence on them.

Each of us is the total sum of the stuff inside—thoughts, habits, and perceptions. It is who we are. We can't fake it. If we want to change, our hearts have to change first.

CHECKPOINTS ✔

Review or discuss this chapter using the following questions.

1. Why is a person's inside stuff so important? What kind of inside stuff do you have?

   _____

   _____

   _____

2. What kind of inside stuff makes up a good friend? Name some specific traits.

   _____

   _____

   _____

3. Do you have friends who help you grow? How?

   _____

   _____

   _____

4. Why are outward actions important in a friendship? How are they related to inside stuff?

_____

_____

_____

5. What fruit do you see in your orchard? Your friends'? What does this tell you about your relationships?

_____

_____

_____

Putting Positive Pressure to Work for You

W hen Will and I started dating," Janet told her friend Jane, "I wasn't interested in joining the band. But Will enjoyed playing so much, I caught on to his enthusiasm. He encouraged me to give it a try, and somehow I got up the courage. How glad I am that I did!

"Today I have a whole new group of friends in addition to my old ones. Instead of going to the mall every weekend, I go to games, get together with other band members to listen to music and practice, and go out in groups with them."

Janet was describing the positive influence dating Will had had on her social life. It wasn't that Will had

Whether our friends are positive or negative, their attitudes tend to rub off on us.

coerced her into the band—he would have dated her even if she hadn't joined. But his natural enthusiasm rubbed off on his girlfriend, and their shared interest drew them closer.

Whether our friends are positive or negative ones, their attitudes tend to rub off on us. We pick up new ideas and interests when people become enthusiastic. When they make something look good, we want to try it too.

Better Peers, Better Future

If you could look down the road of your life and see how your friends would influence you, wouldn't you want to spend most of your hours with the people who would give you good relationships, make you successful in your work, and help you build a good family life? Those elements could make you happy for years.

To some degree, you can start doing that today by taking two steps:

1. Identify your plan. We've talked a lot about having a plan for your life. If you haven't done it already, start to work on your goals. What do you want to be ten years from now? What kind of people do you want to share life with?

For example, when you consider your working life, do you want to:

- Become a journalist
- Work with computers
- Be a tax accountant
- Become a missionary
- Work on machinery
- Become a secretary
- Teach children
- Become a health-care worker

Maybe you don't know just what you want to be yet. Then look at what you like to do. Do you:

- Love to read
- Like to play games with numbers
- Enjoy working on cars in your spare time
- Wish you could spend more time with children
- Like showing people new ideas
- Enjoy making up songs
- Spend all your free time with a computer

Add to those lists. They will give you ideas about the areas you'd be happy in. They can help you decide on a goal to aim for. Next think of how you can begin to achieve that goal. What will you need in education? Whose help will you need? Pick out some people whose positive influence will move you toward your goals.

2. Identify the people you want to influence you. People are an important factor in any plan. They can help you or hurt you, give you information or tear you down.

Once you know where you want to go, you can see the kind of people who can help you.

If you wanted to become a mountain climber, you wouldn't want to spend your time only with people who were afraid of heights (though you might still have some friends who were). You would want to spend your weekends rock climbing or developing other skills that would help you achieve that goal. Someone who had

---

You will sleep better, feel better about yourself, and have more friends if you listen more than you talk, serve more than you expect to be served, and give more than you take.

---

experience in that area could help you a lot. If you wanted to write a book, you'd probably want to meet someone who had done it before. Maybe you'd want to join a group of writers who could rub off on you.

Whatever your goals for the future, you need to spend time around people who can help you achieve your goals—teachers, business people, friends, and so on.

Does that mean you have to choose your friends only for what they can do for your career? No, because not everyone you work with will become very important in your life. You also need friends who can help you grow in character. They may not want to go to college with you, join in the same career, or go to the same church you do, but they may help you become the best person you can be.

"Joanne showed me how to make people my friends," Rita shared. "She's got an outgoing nature, while I'm really quiet. But our friendship has helped me realize that I have to reach out to people first if they are going to feel comfortable with me.

"I may never be able to sell things the way Joanne can, but I can learn to like people more by being around her. I needed to learn that."

Joanne and Rita have a growing friendship because they challenge each other to do their best. "Rita is really sensitive to people," Joanne pointed out. "She knows how not to hurt them in difficult situations. I tend to charge right in sometimes and put my foot in my mouth. Rita has helped me with that."

Though they may not stay such close friends once they leave school, Joanne and Rita have been good influences on each other.

Today commit yourself to developing friendships that challenge you to:

- Learn new skills—through school, hobbies, sports, and so on
- Develop more sensitivity toward people
- Identify ways you can help others
- Draw closer to God through Bible study and prayer
- Become the best person you can be

"Isn't that a selfish attitude?" Morgan wanted to know. "I mean, I don't want to use people."

If you only take from people, you will be using them. So make sure you give, too. As you become a person of integrity, pass that on to your new friends. Share time with them to help them reach their goals. Go new places with them so that they can reach out to others. But don't let it stop there.

Your Mark on the World

When I get to heaven, I want to have been one of the movers and shakers who really reached the center of God's will and did exactly what God wanted me to do with my life. I can't wait to talk to Moses, Paul, John, Philip, and Noah. Knowing the giants of the faith will give me a real charge.

What you do today is important, so live faith to the fullest and make your life the best it can be. Enjoy life, because there is too much going on for you to sit around and feel sorry for yourself. But keep your eye on the end God has prepared for you.

A few years ago, I was challenged to write out a list of goals I have never accomplished. Two of the things I

A dream is something you'd like to do; a goal is a specific thing that you've planned how to do.

put on that list were that I had never skied in the Rockies and never gone to Russia to hand out Bibles. Today I have done both of them.

I wrote down the first and made it happen. With the second goal, a friend asked me, I prayed about it, and the doors opened. I knew God was in it. We got to Russia two days after the coup. We were in a scary situation, but we did it anyway.

Make serving others your major goals, and you will get more out of life. Today I can look myself in the mirror and like the man I see there. It wasn't always like that. For the first twenty-eight years of my life, I put myself first. When I did wrong, I lied and covered up. It was not a fun way to live. But I have changed—and you can, too.

You decide if you will serve other people or expect them to pay attention to you and make you feel good. But you will sleep better, feel better about yourself, and have more friends if you listen more than you talk, serve more than you expect to be served, and give more than you take.

When you die, what do you want people to remember about you? Do you want them to say:

"She never thought of anyone but herself."
"He forgot about his family; he didn't have time for them."
"She was always in and out of trouble—it was so sad."
"He may have been cool, but he made a lot of people suffer."
"What does she have to show for her life?"

Or do you want them to say:

"I didn't always agree with him, but I could respect him."

"He's left his children with a wonderful legacy of faith."

"People all over the world loved her."

"She gave a lot to her home, school, and community."

"No one could forget what a wonderful man he was."

"If I could be like anyone, I'd want to be like her."

You can influence the lives of others every day by living by faith, reaching out to hurting people, and dealing lovingly with people. Even if you never become famous, you will earn a proud name and reputation for leading, not following, standing for what is right, and being a person of faith.

Don't only seek to be with people who will put good pressure on you. Reach others with the message that following the crowd is not the only way—or the best way.

You can do it. Go for it!

CHECKPOINTS ✔

Review or discuss this chapter using the following questions.

1. What plans do you have for your future? If you don't have any, start to work on one for your career, your spiritual life, and your personal goals. When you have written down some ideas,

When I want to accomplish a new goal in my life, I try to find some-one who has already accomplished it and can give me good advice.

ask yourself how they relate to the things you like to do. Will you be happy if you can't include some of the things you enjoy doing in your career, home life, and so on?

_____

_____

_____

2. Who can help you choose your best goals? Achieve them? Show your plan to people who can give you a hand and discuss how your goals suit you and how you can accomplish them.

_____

_____

_____

3. How can you avoid using people who help you plan and achieve your goals?

_____

_____

_____

4. What are your goals for touching the world? When you die, what would you like people to remember you for? Write the obituary you would like to see for yourself. What steps can you take to achieve those goals?

_____

_____

_____

No Defenses

After an assembly in Missouri, Mark was waiting for me outside the school. As I headed for the parking lot, he caught up to me.

"May I talk with you, please?" he asked.

"Certainly," I said, though I was on my way to the middle school for the next assembly.

For a few moments we walked away from the crowd of students changing classes. When we were alone, Mark wanted to know, "What is wrong with sleeping with my girlfriend? We've been dating for over two years, and we plan on getting married someday."

"Why are you asking me for advice?" I wondered aloud. He already seemed to have made up his mind.

"Well, your talk kind of got to me. Deep down inside I really don't know what to do. I feel confused. My girlfriend and I were sitting together, and halfway through she pulled her hand away from mine. I could tell she felt convicted by some of the things you were saying— or something I couldn't understand was going on in her head."

"Why are you having sex with her?" I asked.

"Because we love each other, and we have become so close that it is easy, natural, and fun."

I gave Mark a challenge. I knew it would be hard advice, but it was in their best interest. "Have a talk with her," I said. "Talk about respect and honesty— what is right and wrong. Discuss having enough self-discipline to stay away from your own pleasures, even though they feel fun and easy. I challenge you to have that talk and to mutually decide to stop having sex."

"Why?" Mark wanted to know. "We've been doing it for two years. How will it hurt if we keep on?"

I get this question all the time. It's a many-sided problem. I explained to Mark that the longer you become sexually and emotionally involved, the deeper the hurt of a breakup goes. It can damage your self-esteem immensely. So often I get letters from teens who describe the pain of getting sexually involved. They wish they had never started when they experience it over and over again—but they often have trouble stopping.

"You know, there is a good chance you will not marry her," I commented to Mark.

"What do you mean?"

"You have been having sex with her for a couple of years. Soon you are both graduating, and you will meet other people. Once a boy has sex with a girl, it is easy

---

When your heart tells you you've done wrong, you need to listen carefully. Otherwise your heart becomes hard.

---

to feel he has conquered her. She is no longer a challenge, and you start to feel she isn't so desirable.

"Even if you do marry, both of you could always have doubts. I'd encourage you to take my advice from the assembly and become second-chance virgins. Otherwise, when you are away from her, will she really be able to trust you? Will she know you can say no to things that are pleasurable, fun, and easy? A lot of women will see you. If you can't say no now, how do you know you will say no later?

"And while you are gone, will you be able to trust her? What if you learned that she had an affair? It would devastate you both.

"Discover your own moral strength now—not later.

"If you don't marry her," I went on, "when you break up, you will want to have sex with someone else. You have that need now, and you won't want to deny it. Condoms do not perfectly protect you from diseases or keep a girl from getting pregnant—they fail nearly 15 to 30 percent of the time. Only one mistake can ruin your life. Is it worth it?"

I asked how he felt when he went to church.

"I feel real guilty," Mark answered.

"What do you mean?"

"My mom and dad and her parents know we've been dating for two years, but they have no idea we're sexually active. Every Sunday, when we sit together in church, I feel terrible."

"Do you know what that is?" I asked.

"No."

"That is your heart; it's your conscience talking to you," I explained. "God is telling you what is right. You know what you are doing is wrong. By hiding from him and having your sex 'in the dark,' you only make matters worse. You've become callous to the right.

"When your heart tells you you've done wrong, you need to listen carefully. Otherwise your heart becomes hard. Later on God may shout at you to help you avoid trouble, and you may not hear. You could even lose your life because you aren't listening.

"Do you want God's blessing?" I asked.

"Of course."

"You know marriages today are tough. Half of them end in divorce. You'd like God's blessing on your marriage, wouldn't you?"

"I sure would." Mark nodded.

"How can you ask for God's blessing in marriage down the road if today you look him in the eye and say you don't care, and you are going to sin anyway? If that is your attitude toward him, you will not get his blessing on your marriage.

"You are defending what you want to do," I pointed out to him. "Though you know you are wrong, you are trying to talk yourself into believing it is right. Don't build a wall against your conscience," I advised. "Just listen to your heart and do what is right."

In my travels I always avoid any setting where liquor is served because I know my own weaknesses and the dangers that lurk there. I could go in and have a coke while I enjoy the band, but taking a chance that I would yield to temptation is not worth what it would do to my reputation, my family, and my marriage. I have had to turn down speaking engagements because they wanted me to come to the open-bar reception just before I spoke to an adult group.

Overcoming Wrong

I hope Mark and his girlfriend accepted my challenge. They had headed down the wrong path for so long that Mark found it hard to believe he had to turn around. He felt he had to defend his actions, though his conscience was trying to get through to him.

When we do wrong once, our consciences shout to us. It's as if a brass band were blasting our ears, and we feel so bad that we want to stop. But when we enjoy the wrong, we may cover our ears and attempt to ignore the band. We do the same wrong again, and the next time the band doesn't seem so loud. Soon it doesn't sound like a band anymore—it's more like the whine of a mosquito.

Does your conscience sound like a band or a mosquito? Maybe it sounds loudly and clearly when it comes to stealing. You would never think of taking something that belonged to someone else. But you feel comfortable having sex, because it "feels good."

We all have weak points in our lives. God wants to reach us and change our mistakes into righteousness. But when we ignore our consciences, the whine of the insect will not help us turn from the wrong. God will have to use something louder to get our attention.

Sometimes when we face troubles, we have brought them on ourselves by turning our consciences into

---

Does your conscience sound like a brass band or a mosquito?

---

mosquitoes. We feel like partying all weekend long. Our parents yell at us to study, and we ignore them. At first our grades are okay. The C doesn't look too good on a quiz, but it's only one quiz. Nothing too big. When the final comes, so may the crash. The D that results from too many parties and too little studying can ruin a grade-point average. The warnings didn't work, but a bad grade for a semester might.

When you know you are going down a wrong path, don't let your own defensiveness keep you from turning around. Listen to the people who want the best for you. Face the facts that don't feel so pleasant. Come to God for a reminder of right and wrong.

When you fearlessly face the truth, seek God's will, and take action to do it, you will return to the right path. It might seem rocky at first. You may have to climb a few mountains along the way, but soon you'll be running downhill or over a flat plain. Get through the tough part of changing habits, and move beyond the problems.

It will be one of the best decisions of your life.

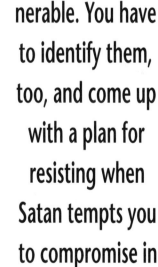

Satan knows your weak areas and where you're vulnerable. You have to identify them, too, and come up with a plan for resisting when Satan tempts you to compromise in those things.

CHECKPOINTS ✔

Review or discuss this chapter using the following questions.

1. Why was Mark so defensive about his actions? What did it show?

_____

_____

_____

2. How does God use our consciences in our lives? What does it mean when your conscience is not telling you anything?

_____

_____

_____

3. Has your conscience ever sounded like a mosquito? Why did it do that? Has it ever sounded like a brass band? What did you do?

_____

_____

_____

4. Is your conscience trying to tell you something today? Does it sound like a band or a mosquito?

_____

_____

_____

5. Can you identify weak points in your life? What keeps you from changing? What can you do about it?

_____

_____

_____

A Blueprint for Life

I f you wanted to build a house, what would you do? Would you walk down the street, turn a corner, and just start building?

No!

Why not?

Because a major project like that takes a lot of planning. First you would have to buy some land and get permission to build. Then you would have to get a contractor, workers, supplies, and so on. You can't just rush into these things.

Well, it's the same thing with your life. You have to plan for success.

What do you want to build? Your life can be:

> A wooden shack
> A straw house
> A teepee
> A pup tent
> A solid brick house
> A palace

It's up to you.

Teens who have thought about their life purposes know how to say no at the right time.

Life Building Quiz

Do you have a plan for your life? What does it consist of? Check all of the following statements that are true about you.

- ❏ I know what I am good at doing and try to build skills in those areas.
- ❏ I can name three people who are positive influences on my life.
- ❏ My friends help me grow by challenging me to do good for others.

❏ I can say no to drugs, alcohol, and sex—and I do.

❏ When others ask my opinion on an important subject, I am not afraid to say what I think and how I feel.

❏ When people disagree with me, I understand that that's okay.

❏ Before I make a choice, I think about it.

❏ When a friend calls, I can say I don't want to go if he has plans to visit a place that would hurt me.

❏ Before I go to movies, I make sure I know what they are about and how they are rated. No X- or R-rated movies are shown before my eyes.

❏ When older people advise me to do something that is against God's Word, I politely refuse.

How many of these did you check?

7–10: *You have most of what you need to build a solid house. You know right from wrong. Start building the house that will suit you best.*

4–6: *You have some of the tools you need, but you need a better blueprint. Strengthen your ideas of right and wrong. Learn to develop plans that will help you build a better future.*

0–3: *Your toolbox is almost empty. No one can read your plans. Tune in to what is right and wrong. Focus on what God's Word has to say, then make plans for a house that will stand.*

Teens who have their life purposes planned know how to say no at the right time. They know how wrong choices could harm them. When they have a choice, they decide they want a castle, not a shack, so they pick up another building block instead of a broken board.

Let's see how three teens focused on their life purposes and made good choices.

Tony heard that the "whole senior class" would be at a graduation party thrown by another senior. "I won't be there," he told his friend Ben. "Vince runs with a tough crowd. I know he had a party last year that got raided by the police. That kind of party seems like it could be a bad mistake."

Tony was right. One girl had a drug overdose and died the night of the party.

Tony planned ahead to make the right decision. Though he knew that "everyone" was going, he didn't feel as if his life would be short-changed if he missed Vince's party. He wanted better things for his future—and he was willing to plan ahead to have them.

At lunch Ron's friend Dexter asked if he could look at his paper during the exam they had next period. Ron didn't want to answer right away, so he put Dexter off. All through lunch, Ron worried. He knew what was right, but how could he tell his friend no? Right up until the test started, Ron thought about all the possibilities. He could fail if they were found out; he could get caught, while Dexter got away. But if he didn't do it, his friends might think he was a wimp. They might even cast him aside.

Just before the test, Ron found the courage to say no to his friend. It was not worth the chance of getting a reputation as a cheater, he decided.

Meg wanted to go shopping, but her mother said no. "You've spent a lot of money this month, and you will need it when you start college. More clothes right now will not pay your bills next September."

When Lee, her best friend, offered to drive to the mall, Meg wanted to go. "Just come and look," Lee suggested. "You don't have to buy anything."

Meg thought about her mother's words. "Nah, if I went, I'd want to spend what I've got. Mom's right—I need to save a little right now. You go on without me."

Having a life purpose takes a lot of planning. If you want to go along and follow the crowd, you don't have to think about it much beforehand. Setting goals and identifying where you want to be will take time, but goals help you have the future you want.

Do you have to have everything in your life tied down in order to have a purpose? No. But you do need to have some ideas about where you are heading.

Setting goals and identifying where you want to be take time, but goals help you have the future you want.

Plan Ahead

Don't wait until you are at the party and everyone is drunk before you decide you should not be there. Don't wait until you are sitting in the back seat and passions flare before you explain your sexual standards. When you are drag racing on the highway, you cannot decide what not to do in a car. Leaving choices to the last minute helps you make mistakes. Setting life-purpose goals and standing up for them ahead of time will help you do what is right.

Recently, at a conference, I met a senior who was telling younger kids to say no to alcohol. April knows what she's talking about when it comes to drinking and driving. She was in an accident, and her face is scarred. She cannot speak properly. Every day she feels the pain that resulted from one wrong choice. She and a friend waited until it was too late to make a decision. Today they regret but cannot change that. So they warn others not to make the same mistake.

When two girls told me of the date rapes they'd suffered from the same boy, it was obvious they'd both waited until too late to say stop. If they had never been alone with him, they could have avoided the pain; if he had learned to say no, he could have avoided the lawsuit the girls brought. Every one of them has bad memories that could last a lifetime.

When you only worry about whether or not others will accept you, you run the risk of much pain. You will never see yourself as special if all you're trying to do is live up to the expectations of friends, acquaintances, and classmates. Peer pressure will eat you alive. When you always want to please other people, you cannot choose the right way and make a stand.

Today sinning is easy. You can go along with the crowd and feel as if you are cool. But who will be with you when you have a sexually transmitted disease, the guilt that comes with an abortion, or a jail sentence for selling drugs? None of the people you tried so hard to impress will hold your hand and go with you into trouble.

You can avoid the pain of all that if you look at your own worth, discover what God has for your future, and aim for it.

Know Your Own Worth

You are different from everyone else. God has given you a special package of skills, interests, and situations. No one can do what you can do in life in just the way you can do it.

Maybe you hate history and love science. Or you find it hard to stay in class but can't wait to get out on the hockey field. Neither is right or wrong—it's just you.

Discover the interests and abilities God has given you. Don't try to force yourself into someone else's mold, because it just won't work.

Discover What God Wants for Your Future

In the Bible God describes some things all Christians should share. He has shown us how to be kind, giving, loving, and so on. By reading your Bible and praying, you can grow in these areas.

But he also has some goals that are just for you. He will help you decide where to go to college and whom

---

God has goals that are just for you. Draw close to him and he'll help you see what they are.

to marry, and he will answer many other questions about your life. As you draw closer to him, you will begin to see the goals he has for you.

As well as becoming the kind of Christian God describes in his Word, you also need to take on the mission he has specifically for you. Whether you are a car mechanic, a teacher, a missionary, or a plumber, you need to do it for him. When you set your sights on his goals, you will become a success, no matter what the world says.

Mission Statements

Lots of businesses have what they call mission statements. In them they define what their goals are and how they plan to reach them. You can have a mission statement for your life—one that can expand with time. When you write one, you don't have to feel as if you can never add to it, remove an idea from it, or change your message. But it will set your sights on something you want to accomplish and give you a sense of direction.

Frieda described her mission statement with these words: "I want to be the best fiction writer I can be. That means I'll have to spend a lot of time at my computer practicing, take as many English courses as I can, and go to college."

"I want to help people come to know God by serving them" was how Carl defined his goal. "Helping the homeless, feeding the hungry, and training people for work are all practical ways I can reach them as I show them the gospel. When I treat them this way, they will see the Good News in action and will want to know the God I serve."

"I'm good at working with my hands, and I enjoy doing it," Joe explained. "When I fix a car, I want it to run well—and I want the person who owns it to know it's right. My reputation is on the line, so I want people to get only the best."

"When people have seen me, I want them to know they have seen Jesus," shared Vicky. "If I'm a housewife or an executive, they should still know that. Whether I'm at home or in the work force, they should see him first."

"I won't be happy if I can't teach," Robert said. "When people's eyes light up and I know they understand how science works, I feel happy. It's what I was meant to do."

All these teens described their mission statements in a few simple words. Each has a future plan that keeps him or her on course. When Frieda doesn't feel like studying, she remembers that she wants to be the best writer ever, and it gives her new energy. When Vicky gets angry, she reminds herself that she isn't looking much like Jesus. If Robert wants to go to a party and someone offers him a drink, he remembers how that could destroy his brain.

Life purposes are simply larger goals that can help you look into the future. When you need to make plans today, they are very helpful. Focusing on tomorrow gives you a better perspective on the people and ideas around you.

CHECKPOINTS ✔

Review or discuss this chapter using the following questions.

1. What kind of plan for success do you have? How would you describe the "house" you're building?

   _____

   _____

   _____

2. Have you ever said no to something because you saw it would not be good in the long run? What happened? Were you glad you said no?

   _____

   _____

   _____

3. Make a list of all the interests and abilities you feel you have.

   _____

   _____

   _____

4. Write a mission statement for your life. Include where you want to go and how you can get there.

   _____

   _____

   _____

To help you decide what goals you should have, make a list of your interests and abilities. Include the things you do easily and enjoy. Also include the things other people seem to notice about you.

Contracts for Living

Purposeful living is goal oriented. Once you know what you want to do, you set up plans and principles that will help you get there. One of the ways you can do that is by using contracts. These will help you plan with other people, agree on what you want to do, and stick to your plans. In this chapter we'll look at some sample contracts that can help you on your way.

I'm a great believer in contracts. When I bought my house, I had to sign a contract so that everyone would know what we were agreeing to. I knew I had to make my payments on time or the bank would take my house away from me. Because of that, every month, I make certain the check is in the mail.

When you buy a car, it's the same thing. You sign a promise that you will pay the bank so much every month. If you don't, they come and repossess your car.

Contracts tell us how much we owe someone and how we have to pay it. They keep us honest, because we know we won't like what will happen if we break the contract. We can see the pain ahead, so we avoid it.

In life, contracts help us know the rules. They can help teens avoid situations that can harm their lives, and they can help them communicate clearly with their parents and other teens.

Driving the Car

Before you step into a car, you should know that it's a very serious action. It can take you where you need to go, or it can end your life. When driving and alcohol interact, the car becomes the number-one teen killer. That's why I encourage teens to make a car contract with their parents.

Teen/Parent Car Contract

As the parent, I promise to do the following things for my driving teen:

1. I will come and get my teen if he/she needs help. My teen can call me anytime, and I will provide a ride home. I will not ask questions but will wait for the truth to come out.
2. I will accept my teen's story as the truth. I will trust my teen to tell me honestly what has happened to and with the car.

3. I will hold my teen to the curfew rules of our household. Broken curfews will be grounds for not using the car for_____.

    (fill in an amount of time)

_____

_____

(Parents' signatures)

As the teen driving the car, I agree to the following rules:

1. I will know what time my curfew is and come home on time. If I run into a problem, I will call ahead.
2. I will not speed. Because I know the laws that govern driving, I understand that speeding is dangerous, and I will not do it.
3. I will not use alcohol or drugs whether or not I am driving, and I will not drive or ride with a teen who uses them.
4. I will use seat belts whenever I am in the car. Because most states have laws for seat belts, I understand that they are required for safety. I want to be a safe driver, so I and my friends will use them in the car.
5. I will not make last-minute changes in plans and call to discuss them with my parents. When I go out the door, I will know where I am going and when I need to return home. Out of respect for my parents, I will hold to these plans except under unusual circumstances. If the plans must be changed, I will call.
6. I will not pick up hitchhikers. I know this is not a safe practice and will avoid it at all costs.

7. I will not leave the car without gas or close to empty. I will pay for the gas I use and other expenses.

8. If I break this contract, I understand that I will lose the privilege of using the car for

_____ .

(fill in an amount of time)

_____

(Teen driver's signature)

I'm not asking parents to suspend their knowledge of their child or the use of their brains when they sign this contract, nor am I expecting teens to suddenly become perfect. But I am asking both to carefully consider the responsibilities that go with driving and to establish the kind of trusting relationship that will make it work.

A driving contract will help both sides understand what is expected and fulfill their obligations. When one side breaks the contract, the other will know what to expect. If there is a question, either side can appeal to the written agreement.

A dating contract will ground teens in good habits.

Dating

When a boy and girl date, they need to understand how they can treat each other well. They need to respect each other physically, spiritually, and emotionally. Going too far sexually, doing things God would not approve of, and belittling each other will not build a strong relationship, and it may damage their whole lives.

That's why I encourage teens to think carefully about the people they date and draw up a contract that will ground them in good habits.

Teen-to-Teen Dating Contract

1. We will treat each other with respect at all times. We will consider each other's physical, spiritual, and emotional well-being on our dates. When we speak to each other, it will be in respectful tones, even if we do not agree on an issue. We will not embarrass each other publicly.

   Physically we will avoid acts that will not please God. We want to keep our relationship pure by saving sex for the marriage relationship. Keeping high expectations for each other will help us plan for a better future.

2. We will not go to places that would compromise our beliefs or morals. We will not go into a house where parents are not home; we will avoid temptation and the rumors that might result. We will not visit places that might harm our reputations.

3. We will not go parking. Heavy petting can lead to trouble, and we do not want that in our lives. Because we are committed to the best for each other, we will avoid encouraging our hormones

    to take over by not putting ourselves in this situation.

4. We will pray before and after each date. Beforehand we will ask that God protect us and that we have a good time. Afterwards we will thank him for our safety and for the respect we have been able to show each other. We do not want to feel pressured by each other or by the expectations of others; instead we want to please God in all things.

5. We will ask others to pray for us. At least one close friend should be praying for us when we go on dates. Having that backup will help us keep up our moral standards.

6. We will report to friends after our dates. We want to have this accountability so that we can challenge each other to do the best on our dates.

7. We will visit with our parents after dates. When we come home we will let them know we have returned safely and that they can trust us. We will give a brief description of what we did and where we went.

8. We will focus on communication. When we go out together, we will try to listen carefully and share honestly.

9. We will make friends part of our dating plans. Because we want to learn to blend in well with a group, we will make plans to go on group dates and meet with groups to have fun.

10. Nothing illegal will take place on our dates. We will not drink or take drugs or break the law in any way.

11. We will not tolerate anything against God's laws on a date. We know when something is wrong

in his eyes, and we will not make it part of our dating life.

12. We will call home if we are going to be late. When a situation makes it impossible to make curfew, we will let our parents know what has happened and when we will be home.

13. We will call our parents if our plans change. Our parents need to know where we are. If our plans change, we will let them know about it when it happens, not at the end of the date. We will not call at the last minute.

_____

_____

(Teens' signatures)

Taking people for granted, treating them without respect, and avoiding right decisions are not the things God has in mind for you.

You want to have growing relationships with others, not damaging ones. That is why you need to sign this agreement and abide by it. If you make a contract such as this, you'll discover that you will:

- Grow socially with the opposite sex and people in general. If you begin dating people who have good values, you'll be able to say no in sticky situations.
- Avoid the pressure to make out that often is part of double dates. When you go out with another couple, if they want to have sex, you will feel as if you must, too. A group situation is safer.
- Learn to talk, listen, and go with the flow. When you marry, you will not have sex all day, every day. But you will need to know how to communicate with your mate and others. Relationships that lack communication fail.
- Do not put yourself in places that will make you compromise physically. When you avoid being alone with each other in a parked car or at a home, you will not take off any of your clothes or let your date touch a part of your body that is not exposed.
- Challenge each other to say no to sex. If you can't say no now, what makes you think you will be able to after marriage if someone else looks desirable? Many people do abstain, despite the stories you hear.

When you damage a date, you damage yourself, too. Instead of doing what is popular, I challenge you to do things God's way. Taking people for granted, treating them without respect, and avoiding right decisions are not what God has in mind for you.

Don't compromise, even when life gets tough. If you take the wide road now, because it seems easy, you will regret it later in life. If you take the narrow road now, you will pay a price in popularity, but tomorrow you will benefit immensely.

Make your own plan for success—following God's agenda.

Don't fall for the ads, the stories, and the peer pressure that push you to do the cool thing. Instead make your own plan for success—following God's agenda. Listen to the people who have your best interests at heart, not those who want to gain from you.

Dating should be fun, and it can be if you do it God's way.

Creating Contracts

Whenever you need someone else's help in knowing where you stand and planning for success, you can make a contract that spells these things out. You can do it by:

1. Identifying the principles. What is right? What do you need to avoid? By knowing where you stand morally, you can pinpoint the things you need to do or keep from doing.

2. Allowing for the other people involved. When you are making a contract, each side has needs and opinions. Discuss what you want to do and where you want to go, considering always what God says is right and wrong.

3. Setting your goals. What do you want to achieve with this contract? With your life? You have to have a goal to shoot for when you contract with someone. If you built a house you would contract for certain dimensions and materials to be used. In the same way, you need a plan for your life.

4. Writing it all down. Put it on paper in the clearest, most specific terms you can develop.

5. Discussing it with your contract partner. Do you both understand what each point means? Unless you agree on what the terms of the contract mean, you will have trouble later.

6. Signing the contract. When you do this, realize that you are agreeing to important terms. Both of you will hold each other to the contract. When you have doubts, you will return to what you have written to decide what to do about the situation.

I'm not suggesting that you write a contract for everything you do in life. You could get bogged down in paper if you did that. But when you face a serious situation that involves other people, a contract can help you plan for success and give you extra motivation to do the right thing.

Make your life positive, hopeful, and helpful by looking ahead and planning to do right. Contracts are only part of that, but they can mean a lot to you.

Relationships can be wonderful when everyone involved has the same expectations and follows the same set of rules.

CHECKPOINTS

Review or discuss this chapter using the following questions.

1. What do contracts do? Why are they important?

_____

_____

_____

2. Read over the Teen/Parent Car Contract. Do you
   agree with all that is written there? Why or why
   not? Would you have a hard time keeping to
   this agreement? Why?

   _____

   _____

   _____

3. How would you feel about asking a regular date
   to sign the dating contract? Would it be a problem? What does that tell you about your dating
   relationship?

   _____

   _____

   _____

4. Why is dating such an important relationship?
   What can you gain from it? Lose in it? How can
   you avoid trouble?

   _____

   _____

   _____

5. Do you need to make some other contracts with friends, family, or people in your community? What points would the contract need to cover? Make up a sample one that you can discuss with the other person.

_____

_____

_____

This Could Be Habit-Forming

ollow the crowd? No one knows what it means to do that better than I do. Until I was about thirty, I rarely acted independently. When other people told me to drink, I drank. If a friend wanted to do drugs, I went along.

But one day I looked in the mirror and did not like the man I saw.

I could excuse a lot of what I did with the fact that I did not have the best home life. My parents had so many problems that they did not have enough love for us six kids. I grew up craving attention. To get it I always tried to be the funny kid. I joked all the time—and I helped others with their problems. Still I wasn't happy.

For all the efforts I'd made to make people like me, it didn't fill the gap in my life. Though I'd tried to help people, it didn't solve my need for love.

If you are looking for love, you won't find it by going along with the crowd. Why not? Because the crowd just doesn't have the answers you need. Drinking will not fill your empty heart; neither will drugs. I know, because I tried both. They didn't work for me, and they won't work for you either.

A temptation will not give up its hold on your life without a fight, but the daily choices you make can loosen its grip. Each time you make a right decision, God's Spirit expands within you and the old self recedes a little.

From Head to Heart

"What am I doing wrong?" Chris wanted to know. "I changed my friends and focused on the positive, but I still haven't become the person I want to be. I have it in my head, but I don't seem to have it in my heart. Am I weird or something?"

Chris isn't weird, and neither are you if you have a problem changing over to the good things in life. What if you have filled your head with all the right ideas, taken some helpful steps, and asked others for advice, and you still have trouble avoiding peer pressure? Is there a solution? Yes, I believe there still is hope. What you need to do is form some new habits based on the new ideas you've chosen for your life.

When I asked Jesus to take over my life, his Spirit filled the hole that drinking, drugs, and sex never could. Now I could begin to feel loved and love others the way he wanted. I could make choices that healed my past and helped my future. But following Jesus is a lifelong path; everything wasn't made perfect in a flash.

Some things did change right away in my life. I flushed my alcohol down the toilet, promising myself I would never touch it again. But other things took a while to take hold in my life. Anger, sexual temptation, and other areas still challenge me today, but I have taken steps against them, and they present smaller threats to me as I replace the old beliefs with new ones that keep me on God's path.

Each temptation will not give up its hold on your life immediately, but the daily choices you make can loosen its grip. Each time you make a right decision, God's Spirit expands within you and the old self recedes

O ur thoughts are at the center of who we are and they determine our actions. My actions change depending on how I'm thinking at the moment. If I'm in a bad mood and someone looks at me the wrong way, I'm ready to deck them. If things aren't going well and I receive some bad news while I'm already a little depressed, then it's easy for me to get bummed out. If I don't start out my day by spending time with the Lord to get my thoughts straight, the day doesn't go smoothly.

a little. It may take a long time to see a change—but don't give up!

Creating New Habits

Morris told his friends he was not going to shoplift anymore. But he still went to the mall with them. Before long, he was joining them again; he liked the thrill of getting something for nothing—when no one knew what he had done.

Eva decided to give up drugs. But a little while after she made that decision, she went to a party with Sonja. Before the night ended, she did what she had sworn not to do.

Mark wanted to make good grades, but instead of hitting the books each weekend, he went out to play soccer with his friends.

We need to focus on the things we have accomplished and the goals that are important to us.

Sherry promised her Sunday school teacher she would memorize a Bible verse every day. When it came time to read her Bible, Sherry felt too tired. *I'll do it later,* she told herself the first night. Her new habit never got started, because it seemed like too much effort.

All of these teens meant to make a new habit work for them, but they couldn't hold it together in practice. Why? When they made the first choice, they meant it. They knew what was wrong in their lives, and they wanted better for themselves.

Sure, they made the choice mentally, and that was good. But it takes more than that. Let's look at some truths that will help our wishes become reality in our lives.

1. We need to truly want to turn over a new leaf. Mark wanted good grades because his dad had pressured him to do better in school. His father nagged him every day about his schoolwork and told people how bad his grades were. But deep down, Mark didn't understand why he should take time from sports to improve his grades. After all, didn't only wimps study all the time? He wasn't like them.

Mark's real feelings showed up in what he did. No one had given him positive reasons to hit the books, and the pain his dad's comments caused didn't outweigh the fun he had playing soccer. Which gave him the greater motivation? The fun time with his friends, of course.

Before Mark will give up time with his sport, he will need a positive goal that encourages him to study.

2. We need to know that we can do it. Eva was doing well giving up drugs until Sonja pointed out a friend. "See Pat?" she said. "He tried to give up drugs too. For about a year he didn't do any stuff, but finally he went back to it. Do you think you are better than Pat?"

Discouraged at the thought that she was wasting her time combating drugs, Eva gave in.

Without some hope, we slide back into bad habits. Instead of surrounding ourselves with people who tell us we can't, we need positive people who will encourage us to do our best. We need to focus on the things we have accomplished and the goals that are important to us.

3. We need to give ourselves time to develop the new habit. Morris spent a few days away from his shoplifting friends, but he felt so lonely that he called them up again. Instead of giving himself time to make friends who could help him, he returned to the past. If he had waited to feel at home with others, he could have developed the habits he wanted.

When you make a change in your life, you have to keep it up for at least three weeks before it can become a habit. Long after that you may still feel tempted to return to an old way of life. Patience with yourself can help you overcome this.

4. We need to avoid an "I owe myself" attitude. When Eva did not do drugs for a while, she began to feel

When you make a change in your life, you have to keep it up for at least three weeks before it can become a habit. Be patient with yourself!

self-righteous. *I've been so good for so long. Where has it gotten me?* she asked herself when Sonja told her about Pat. Because she already felt sorry for herself, she could not stand up to the pressure.

Feeling sorry for ourselves, thinking we deserve something, and other self-righteous attitudes will not lead to improved lives. These thoughts will only make us vulnerable.

Attack back when "woe is me" hits by praying, promising yourself a better future, looking to the long-term benefits, and seeing how far you have come. Don't let negatives stop you by playing upon your emotions.

5. *We need to ask for support.* Eventually Sherry went to her Sunday school teacher and admitted she was having a hard time memorizing verses. Together they worked out a simpler plan and an earlier time for study, so that Sherry would not feel so burdened. "I will pray

for you," her teacher promised. "Learning God's Word is important, and he will help you do it."

We don't have to go it alone. Plenty of people can understand why new habits are hard to build and will be willing to help us tackle them.

The motives behind our actions are really the beliefs we carry with us. Mentally, we invest in things that make us feel good or bring us some kind of benefits. When our hearts and minds aren't moving in the same direction, we need to take a deeper look at the beliefs that drive them. We'll do that in the next chapter.

Be positive about your ability to change! Be around people who will encourage you.

CHECKPOINTS ✔

Review or discuss the chapter using the following questions.

1. What was Chris doing wrong when he could not change his lifestyle? What was he doing right?

   _____

   _____

   _____

2. What influence do ideas have on our actions? How can we use them to help us toward better actions?

   _____

   _____

   _____

3. Has your heart ever gone in one direction and your mind in another? What happened to you? Did you overcome that problem? How?

   _____

   _____

   _____

4. When we want to start new habits, what attitudes do we need to cultivate? To avoid?

_____

_____

_____

The Belief Gap

The real basis of the choices we make is the ideas that lie behind them. How we act is determined by the way we really think, the things we believe in. And those aren't always as obvious as they might seem.

"I claimed to have it all together," Nadia said. "People thought that I did. They saw my good grades, all my class activities, and so on. What they didn't know was that Ron and I were having sex regularly.

"I knew it was wrong, but once I got started, it was hard to stop.

"In class I felt as if I were running a race I couldn't get out of. Achieving meant that much to me. My par-

How we act is determined by what we think and what we believe in.

ents wanted me to get into a good college, so they encouraged me to do well in school, take on activities, and so on. I wanted that too, so I aimed high, believing that success would make me happy. The problem was, in all the busyness of my life, I felt lonely. I wanted someone to care just for me.

"I thought Ron did that. When we first had sex, I felt uncomfortable with it, but it also made me feel loved, and I needed that feeling. We kept doing it, despite my doubts.

"On the outside my life said, 'I have it all together; I have a positive attitude and can do what I want.' On the inside it was another matter.

"When Ron and I left for different colleges, we wanted to keep our relationship alive, but we also agreed to give each other the freedom to date others. What I didn't count on was that Ron would find someone else and I wouldn't.

"At Thanksgiving break, Ron told me he didn't want to see me anymore. He'd met a girl at his school, and they were pretty serious.

"'We wanted to get married, didn't we?' I couldn't hold back that cry. 'Do you think I would have had sex with you if I thought we were going to break up?'

"He told me he couldn't ruin both our futures just because we'd had sex. When he said that, I felt my life was already destroyed.

"It's taken me a long time to get back on course after losing Ron, but I have done it. One of the big changes is that I feel better about myself now. I know I don't need sex to have love.

"My parents and I have talked a lot about achievement. They understand that the pressure almost made me nuts and that I need a balanced life. That includes love from them and time with other people."

Nadia learned that deep down she didn't really believe achievement was her highest goal. Her empty heart kept track—she needed attention from someone. Ron stepped into her life when she was most vulnerable. The short-term gain did not solve Nadia's problem, however.

"I learned that all the external success did not mean I was whole. Inside I felt a lot of doubts about myself. If I had thought more highly of myself, I might have been able to say no to Ron—and to a lot of pain," Nadia admitted.

When we face choices, we begin to learn what we *really* believe. How easily we say no to what is wrong and yes to what is right shows what we think of ourselves, others, and our faith in God.

Like Nadia, I know what it means to hide behind a mask. As a teen, when I joked around and helped others, I might have seemed as if I really liked people. The problem was that there was one person I didn't think had much value—me.

> I spent most of my life putting on masks and trying to be someone else, acting the way I thought others wanted me to. It's a very hard way to go through life. When I became somewhat successful I put on more masks because I thought people expected me to be a perfect parent, a perfect spouse, and a perfect Christian. I found out that's not what real life is and it's easier and more fun to be real than to be fake. I also found that people like and respect me when I'm myself.

We can put on masks, hide our own opinions of ourselves and others, and try to avoid the truth about our real beliefs, but sooner or later they will come to the front of our lives.

"I say I love God," Erin told me. "But sometimes I open my mouth and say things I know would make him cry. Before I can catch myself, I'm criticizing my friends or putting them down."

Erin's words show there's something inside her that does not agree with her profession of faith. That doesn't mean she doesn't love God, but something in her is not yet willing to do what he commands. She needs to identify what the problem is and let God help her with it.

From Belief to Action

Actions will often reveal what you believe, and they will be hard to change until you change the belief system that goes with them.

You can't separate what you believe and what you do. When you believe in something, you take action based on that belief. When you see the results of that action, you feel good or bad about it. If you feel good, you will repeat the action. If you feel bad, you will try a new belief that will get you out of the cycle.

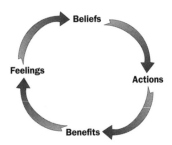

What happens if you can see that you are doing wrong but you get feelings of enjoyment from your actions? You will have to experience enough negatives from your choices to make it worthwhile for you to change your beliefs and the habits they cause. You'll also need positive encouragement to make the change.

What Do You Believe?

What you really believe comes out in the person you are, what you enjoy, and the things you do. Though you may try to put on a mask and pretend to the world that you are what you aren't, or even convince yourself you are one thing when you really are another, the truth comes leaking out.

To hear Walt talk, you would think he always makes the right choices. He has an opinion about everything—how things should be done and who should do them. More often than not he wants to do them, because he has the idea that he is always right and others are always wrong.

But Walt has a "secret" drinking problem. The problem is that it's only a secret to him. Others have warned him about the effect it could have on his life, but he ignores their efforts. He can't see that he doesn't have his life in order. Though he wants to tell others how to act, he needs to get his own act together first.

Marilyn tells other people how much God loves them and that he has forgiven their sins once they believe in Jesus. Yet her own spiritual life is very rigorous and unforgiving. Unless she spends an hour in Bible study and a half hour in prayer every day, she feels guilty. In addition, she tries to tell at least two people a day about God.

"I really messed up last week," she told her youth pastor. "I only talked to five people about Jesus." What she doesn't know is that people avoid her because she treats witnessing as if she were getting notches on a gun. Her lack of real love for them turns people off.

Walt and Marilyn are speaking one way, but their actions clearly show that they believe something else. Though Walt talks about making right choices and is

The gentle correction of loving people can help us redirect our lives.

We need to make a pact with ourselves and God that we'll stay true to our beliefs

very demanding of other people, his own addiction proves that he cannot live up to the rules he would like to impose on himself and others.

Marilyn does love Jesus, and mentally she knows God has forgiven her. The problem is that she hasn't brought that realization fully into her life yet. Because she cannot forgive herself for some things she did before she knew Jesus, she tries to earn his love by talking to others, spending hours in prayer, and reading the Bible.

Are you like Walt and Marilyn? Do you hide the truth from yourself, while others can plainly see it? That's part of the reason I encourage teens to talk to the people who love them most. Sometimes we need an outside view of where we are going and what we are really like inside. The gentle correction of loving people can help us redirect our lives—and though it's painful, it hurts a lot less than the harsh condemnation of those who do not know us well and do not care about our futures.

Belief Discovery Quiz

To discover a few of your inside beliefs, complete the following statements. Where appropriate, fill in more than one answer. Answer honestly, using your whole imagination and your real desires.

1. My greatest success in life is:

2. I feel proudest about this accomplishment:

3. If I could do anything in life, I would:

4. I most enjoy:

5. If I could change anything in my life, it would be:

6. If I could change anything about myself, it would be:

7. When I get mad at myself, it is because:

8. I am least proud about (fill in an activity in your life):

9. My greatest need in life is:

How do others see you?

1. When people talk about me, they say:

2. When people tell me I have done wrong, they point out:

3. When people support me, they say:

4. My friends would describe my strongest point as:

5. My friends would describe my weakest point as:

6. My family encourages me to:

7. My family objects that I:

In a short paragraph, describe what you really think and feel about:

1. Your family

2. Other people

3. Your future

Evaluating Your Answers

From these questions, can you see that your actions, the way you think, and the things you enjoy show what you really believe? Your answers describe what is truly important in your life.

When you took the test, did you discover any themes that came up often in the things you enjoy doing, the objections you hear from others, or the positive things they say to you? Have you taken these ideas seriously? Do you really believe in them? Things that come up repeatedly in your life are more likely to be true. For example, when your teachers tell you they see a lot of unused potential in you, it's unlikely that they are all just telling you that to make you feel good. You may not be working up to your best level, and they can see the person you could be if you put more effort into schoolwork.

Be aware of the biases of people, though. "My parents always told me I was 'too religious,'" Julio remarked. "They wanted me to drop out of youth group and stop going to church. They didn't like the church I was going to and blamed everything I did wrong on my association with it. I talked to my pastor about that, because I didn't want to make a wrong choice.

"When we discussed how my parents felt, my pastor suggested that I try a different tack with them. I'd spent a lot of time telling them about Jesus, but I hadn't lived up to those standards.

"Now I try to witness with deeds more than words. I've tried to be a responsible son to my parents. Though they haven't accepted Jesus yet, they no longer tell me not to go to church. In fact they encourage me."

Julio's parents weren't really against his churchgoing. They simply didn't like his dogmatic attitude that was not backed up by loving actions. With his pastor, Julio found a way to satisfy both himself and his parents.

Evaluate your own weaknesses, the ideas others have about you, and the future you want to create for yourself. If you need help identifying problem areas, talk to a trusted teacher, pastor, or family member. Explain that you want to discover the beliefs that harm your life, and ask them to gently tell you what they see.

How to Change Beliefs

You have identified beliefs that harm your life. Maybe some of them have been subtle—or they may have been so obvious you didn't have to think much to find them. Now what can you do to kick them out of your life?

Let's follow Nadia through a plan she used to change her attitudes.

1. Identify the problem. Nadia's problem was that deep inside she felt lonely. For a while, with achievements to keep her busy and with Ron to give her the affection she craved, she was able to hide from the loneliness.

Whatever it takes to stand firm against peer pressure and improve your life, do it!

But losing Ron brought all her isolated, unloved feelings to the surface. "Achieving seemed the way to make people love me. But it entered me into a race I felt I couldn't stop, and I still didn't feel loved."

2. Identify the thoughts behind the problem. "The problem was really me. I felt as if people only loved me when I got the best grades, went out for the most activities, and went to the 'right' school. I got caught up in all that, I couldn't see that my value as a person was based not on what I did but on what I was. At heart, I didn't think people could love me for myself."

3. Identify how your thoughts need to change. "I had to learn to love myself first," Nadia explained. "Until I did so, nothing else would work. I had to be able to love myself just as I was—warts and all."

4. Figure out a plan that will work. "To love myself I had to learn more about how God loved me, who I was, and how to relate to other people. I got involved in a Bible study on who I was in Jesus. It got rid of a lot of doubts I'd had. Suddenly I knew who I was, because I knew what God said about me. But I had to spend time thinking about the things I did, praying over them, and getting the input of others. That meant spending time with other people, building up a firm social life, and making new friends.

5. Support a new way of thinking. "I was so used to thinking I had to do things that it was hard to relax. But I stayed with my Bible study group when they went on to a new topic. I had shared my problem with two people there, and they committed to praying for me and helping me build a better social life. When I started dating again, we went over the Scriptures that could help me stand firm. Then I promised to call them and talk over my dates after each one."

6. Stand firm when troubles come. "Saying no isn't easy sometimes. I stopped dating one boy who insisted that we have sex, but the peace in my life is worth it. I know there will be other dates. Someday I want to be able to stand before my husband knowing that I waited for him. And now I know that I can do it."

You want to change the beliefs that harm you, and that's the first step. But remember they won't change overnight. If you are hiding the truth of your problems or your real emotions from yourself, it may take a while to discover what's eating you. Nadia's problem wasn't really that she was having sex; that was just the way she responded to the problem. Because she did not love herself, she became open to having sex to get the love she needed. Once you have identified the problem, try to deal with it. Perhaps you need to seek out a pastor or counselor, or maybe you simply need to take action. Whatever it takes to stand firm against peer pressure and improve your life, do it!

Reach inside your
soul to discover
what is important
to you. By doing
this you discover
who you are
inside. It helps
you believe in
yourself and
stand up for
yourself in this
world.

CHECKPOINTS ✔

Review or discuss the chapter using the following questions.

1. Do you have trouble identifying your real beliefs? Why? What can you do about it?

_____

_____

_____

2. Why do people put on masks? Have you ever done this? What was the result?

_____

_____

_____

3. What is the relationship between beliefs and actions? How do benefits and feelings relate to them?

_____

_____

_____

4. What happens when a person acts one way but believes something else? How can you avoid that?

_____

_____

_____

5. What did you discover about your beliefs? Were they what you expected, or did you learn something new about yourself? Do you need to make some changes?

_____

_____

_____

The Beginning of the Story

Where you go in life will depend largely on the choices you make. It's up to you: You can become the kind of person who makes the right choices and develops good relationships with friends, family, and the community—or you can party today and wallow in regrets tomorrow. You can become:

- The girl who is in demand for one-night stands but not for marriage
- The boy who has lost his reputation for honesty and never tries to earn it back
- The woman who has a child born with deformities because she used drugs in high school
- The man who is dying of AIDS because he slept around

Or you can become:

- The guy who never has a million dollars but spends his money wisely
- The girl who has people to support her when times are tough, because she supported them when they needed it

- The woman who has a happy marriage because she said no to sex when she was a teen
- The man who is proud of his work and can support his family without having to become a workaholic

Will you do what is easy—or what is right? Do you want to feel good about yourself? Or ashamed of who you are? Your actions today can start you on a permanent, positive lifestyle.

Every day you have to choose between right and wrong. My kids had a fight the other day. We had the usual ugly family scene for a while. When I talked to them about it later, they tried to tell me, "But God planned it." I told them they were wrong. Though many people seem to think that because he knows the future, God wanted them to sin, they are mistaken. God has given us the freedom to make choices. He also has given us a wisdom base that helps us know the difference between right and wrong.

God does not orchestrate evil. You can't get out of your wrong choices by trying to blame him. God has blessed me with a happy family because I have followed his way. It could so easily have been otherwise.

Do what is right because it is right, because it will benefit you, and because it will enable you to help others.

Who would trade that for all the popularity in the world?

Not until you understand who you are, what you believe, and why you do what you do, will you be able to truly stand up for yourself. Your future can be great—God intended it that way. He has placed you and your talents in a certain spot, in a certain family, in a certain town to accomplish certain things that only you can do. Unless we stand up for who we are and what is right we will not be all God wants us to be.

I care about you. While I want you to care deeply about others, first and foremost I want you to care about you. I said it many different ways in this book, but I want to end with this—You are worth it! You are special!

God bless you.

Your friend,

Bill Sanders

If this book has touched your life, if you need to share a joy or a pain, if you would like a list of my other books and cassettes, or if you want to know how to bring me to speak to your school or group, write me at this address:

BILL SANDERS
P.O. Box 711
Portage, Michigan 49081